# This Moving Activity Journal Belongs To

_____

### On The Move

Moving is exciting, such a big change,
There's so much that I need to do!
I'm packing-up all of my favorite stuff,
And heading to someplace new!
My future is full of discovery,
Happy memories and stories to share.
So I'll journal, plan, dream, and explore
On my move from here to there!

My Moving Activity Journal
Activities, Games, Crafts, Puzzles, Scrapbooking, Journaling, and Poems for Kids on the Move
Second Edition
Written & Illustrated by: Nicole L.V. Jaeger
Edited by: Jacquelyn Wavrunek, www.jacquelyngraphics.com
© 2007 Nicole L.V. Jaeger, Flemington, New Jersey (U.S.A.)
All rights reserved. No part of this book may be transmitted or reproduced in any form by any
means without permission in writing from the publisher.
ISBN 978-0-9796547-0-1
A Soaring Moon LLC Book
SAN 854-0241
Flemington, New Jersey
www.ActivityJournals.com
www.SoaringMoon.com

Volume Sales: For information on wholesale or volume sales, please contact Soaring Moon LLC at orders@soaringmoon.com or visit www.soaringmoon.com.

# My Moving Activity Journal

Activities, Games, Crafts, Puzzles, Scrapbooking,
Journaling, and Poems...for Kids on the Move!

Second Edition

**by Nicole L.V. Jaeger**

**edited by Jacquelyn Wavrunek**

*Soaring Moon LLC*
**www.SoaringMoon.com**

# How to use this Moving Activity Journal

Moving is a big change!  It is also a unique opportunity to learn positive ways for getting through big changes. This Activity Journal provides opportunities for children and families to transition to a new home through exploring, creating, playing, planning, learning, helping, working together, sharing feelings, and most importantly, *having fun!*

**Moving should be an opportunity to thrive, not something to survive!**

## Each person can keep his or her own activity journal...

- For older children who want to explore independently;
- For children who prefer to complete projects by themselves or journal privately;
- For children who want their own moving scrapbook to save for years to come.

## Or, everyone moving can share one activity journal.

- For younger children who need some extra help;
- For children who prefer to work on projects together;
- For families who are moving soon and want to complete the activity journal quickly by working together. (Each person can use his or her own color pen or pencil to show which journal entries belong to him or her.)

## What parents can do:

- **Keep communication open**:  Ask your child to share his or her journal entries and activities, then talk about your own thoughts and feelings too.
- **Empower young movers**:  Encourage and reward your child's help, exploration, and discovery.
- **Facilitate your child's transition**:  Offer as much help as needed, while letting your child work independently as he or she is willing and able.
- **Help make moving fun and creative**:  Use this Activity Journal!

# Adaptable to Different Ages

## Young Readers, Young Adults, and Up

- Consider providing a Moving Activity Journal for each of your older children.
- Encourage your child to talk with you about his or her journal entries and activities.

## Early Readers

- Answer questions and guide your child as needed, encouraging your child to share his or her journaling with you.
- Browse the activities for those which your child will be most successful working on with some help and those that will encourage conversation between you and your child. Use these for valuable one-on-one time that will help your child with his or her big transition. Friends, sitters, and older children can help with these activities too.

## Pre-Readers

- Consider sharing one Moving Activity Journal for all of your pre-readers.
- Guide your child to specific activities that are appropriate for the time allowed and your child's abilities. Find activities that fit your child's current interests, like answering questions about the new home, helping with packing, or wondering what might happen to friends or a pet after the move. Encourage older children to help younger children.
- **Tips for adapting reading-based activities to pre-readers are provided on pages 136 and 137.**

## Keep journaling safe and fun...

- Remind young journalers of all the important rules that need to be remembered when completing these activities, like asking before going outside or using scissors, or only using glue in certain areas, or waiting for a parent before meeting new neighbors, and so on! You know your children, home, and move the best, so modify any activities as appropriate and use common sense precautions.

# Look for These Activities

Journal Entries

Explore, Discover, and Learn New Things

Geography - Finding Fabulous Facts

Arts and Crafts

Games and Puzzles  (Answers are on page 138.)

TIP!  Look for this symbol - you will find suggestions for completing activities or sharing this activity journal.

# Table of Contents

**Look Who's Moving!** ............................................................................13

    We Are Moving ...............................................................................14

    The Home That I am Moving Away From .......................................16

    Secret Place ....................................................................................16

    I Never Noticed That Before! .........................................................17

    Floor Plan ......................................................................................18

    Floor Plan Maze ............................................................................19

    Scrapbook: This is Where I Lived Before I Moved .......................20

    Goodbye Home ...............................................................................22

    Memory Stone ................................................................................23

**Remembering My Schools** ...................................................................24

    Scrapbook: My Schools ..................................................................25

    School Word Search Puzzle ...........................................................27

**Remembering My Community** ..............................................................28

    Community Maze ............................................................................29

    Leafing, a Pressing Matter ............................................................30

    Scrapbook: My Community ............................................................32

**Our Moving Plans** ...............................................................................34

    A Good Reason to Move .................................................................35

    Geography ......................................................................................36

**Our Route** ...........................................................................................37

    Moving Makes Me Feel ..................................................................38

    A Few Thoughts About Moving .....................................................38

    I Need a Break! .............................................................................39

    Keys ...............................................................................................40

**My Research** ......................................................................................41

    Resources .......................................................................................41

    State to State .................................................................................42

My New State .................................................................................43

United States Word Scramble .........................................................44

My Home Inspections .....................................................................46

Rumor Has It... ...............................................................................48

So Much to Look Forward To ..........................................................50

Fun Things to Do Near My New Home ............................................51

Making Myself at Home ...................................................................52

**My New School** ..............................................................................54

Visiting My New School ..................................................................55

Notes About My New School ..........................................................56

Pen Pal ..........................................................................................57

Scrapbook: My New School .............................................................58

**My New Community** ........................................................................60

Making Connections .......................................................................60

People, Places, and Things .............................................................61

Making New Friends .......................................................................62

Friendship Word Scramble ..............................................................63

**Staying in Touch** ...........................................................................64

My Friends .....................................................................................64

So Many Ways to Stay in Touch .....................................................65

I Will Remember You When ...........................................................65

Goodbye Friends ............................................................................66

Post Office Change of Address .......................................................67

Change of Address Cards ...............................................................67

To Do: My Friends Checklist ...........................................................68

My Address Book ............................................................................69

Moving Messages ...........................................................................74

Scrapbook: My Friends ...................................................................76

Game: A Funny Letter .................................................................................... 78

**Packing** .................................................................................................... 80

Where are My Boxes? Stickers ...................................................................... 81

Labeling Boxes .............................................................................................. 82

That's My Most Important Box! ...................................................................... 83

Pack Facts ..................................................................................................... 84

My Packing Plan ............................................................................................ 86

Packing by Definition ..................................................................................... 88

Packing Word Search Puzzle ......................................................................... 89

Packing My Moving Bags ............................................................................... 90

Family Moving Bags ....................................................................................... 92

Packing Ideas ................................................................................................ 93

Jobs for Packing Helpers ............................................................................... 94

Safe Packing Word Scramble ........................................................................ 96

**Safety First** ............................................................................................... 97

Emergency Information .................................................................................. 97

My Moving Safety Card .................................................................................. 98

**Pets on the Move** ..................................................................................... 99

Scrapbook: My Pets ....................................................................................... 100

Pets Moving to a Different Home ................................................................... 102

Pet Facts ....................................................................................................... 103

Moving Pets ................................................................................................... 104

Planning Ahead .............................................................................................. 104

Pet Tags ......................................................................................................... 104

**Moving Day!** ............................................................................................. 105

Moving Day Job # 1 - Double Check ............................................................. 105

Moving Day Job # 2 - My Things ................................................................... 106

Moving Day Job # 3 - Goodbye Walk ............................................................ 106

What I Did the Day We Left ........................................................................... 107

**While Traveling - Some Things to Think About** ........................................108

    Planning Box Crafts .................................................108

    Traveling Maze .......................................................109

    Traveling Word Scramble ..........................................110

    Traveling Word Search Puzzle ................................... 111

    Traveling Observations ............................................112

    Game: A Funny Story ..............................................113

    Moving Travels ......................................................115

**Arriving** ................................................................116

    My Moving Story .....................................................117

    A Picture is Worth a Thousand Words ..........................119

**Settling In** ............................................................120

    Discovering My New Home .........................................121

    All Five Senses .....................................................122

    A New Perspective .................................................123

    Reminder .............................................................123

    The History of My New Home .....................................124

    Neighborhood Hunt .................................................126

    A Trip Around Town ................................................128

    Notes About My New Town .......................................129

    Post Cards ...........................................................130

**What I Have Learned** ...............................................131

    End Notes ...........................................................132

**Tips for Assisting Pre-readers** ...................................136

**Answers** ...............................................................138

**Acknowledgements** ..................................................139

**TIP!** **Getting Started:** Look through the activities before you get started. Some you might want to do right away, others before you move, and some you will save until after you move. Fill the pages in any order that you like. Color the black and white drawings and add your own artwork!

# Look Who's Moving!

(Check One Box)

☐ This activity journal is just for me:

My name is: _____.

I am _____ years old, and I have moved _____ times before.

☐ We are sharing this activity journal:

Name _____Age _____ I have moved _____ times.

Name _____Age _____ I have moved _____ times.

Name _____Age _____ I have moved _____ times.

Name _____Age _____ I have moved _____ times.

Name _____Age _____ I have moved _____ times.

Name _____Age _____ I have moved _____ times.

Name _____Age _____ I have moved _____ times.

Name _____Age _____ I have moved _____ times.

Name _____Age _____ I have moved _____ times.

If you are sharing this journal, write each person's name below, pick a different color for each person, and write the color that will be used for his or her journal entries.

Name: _____ My color is: _____

Name: _____ My color is: _____

Name: _____ My color is: _____

Name: _____ My color is: _____

Name: _____ My color is: _____

Name: _____ My color is: _____

Name: _____ My color is: _____

Name: _____ My color is: _____

Name: _____ My color is: _____

# We Are Moving

Draw or paste pictures of everyone who is moving.

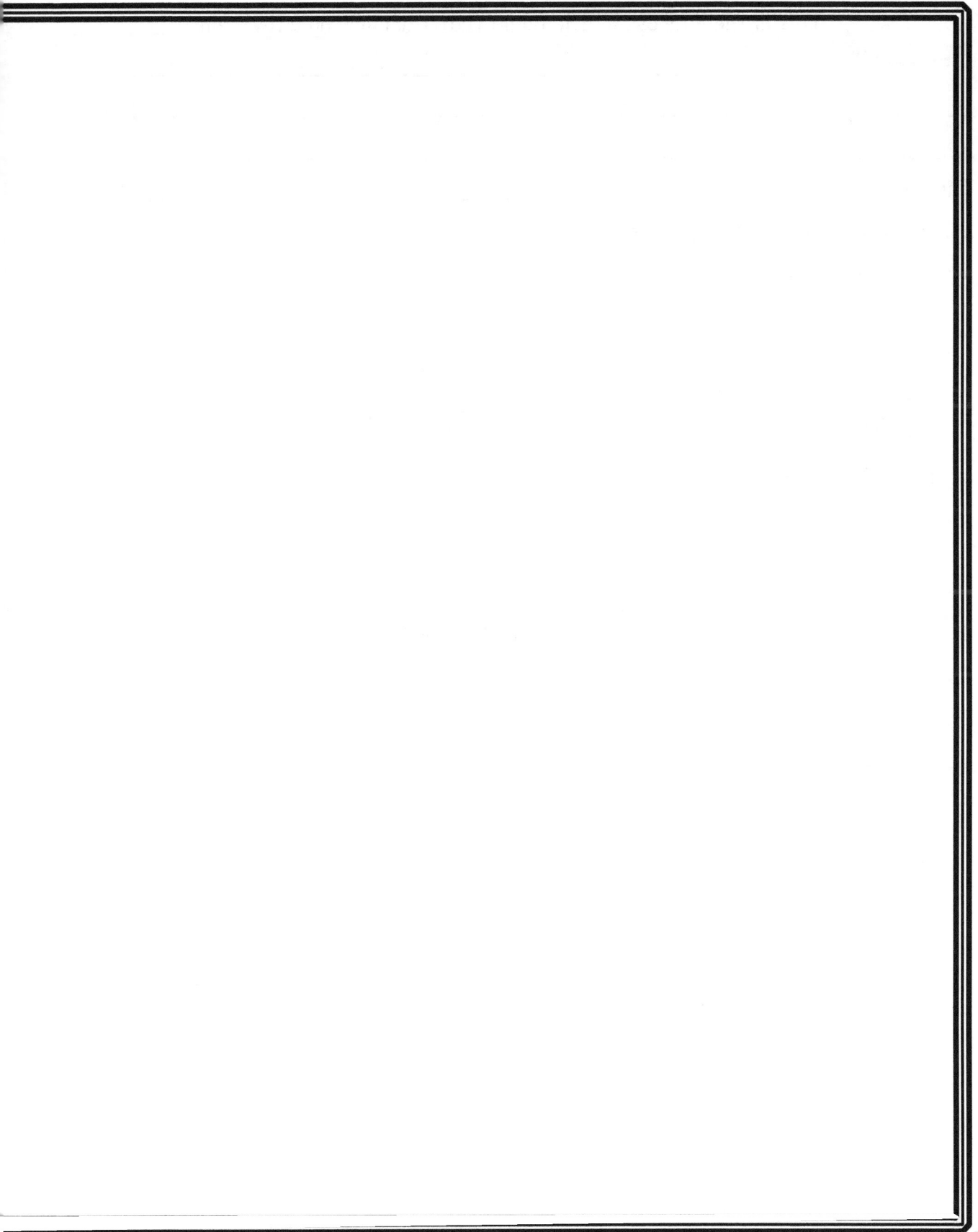

# The Home That I am Moving Away From

This is the address of the home that I am moving away from_____

_____

_____

The phone number is _____

I lived in this home for _____ years.

This home was built in the year _____ and is _____ years old.

This home is:   (Check One)

☐ Very old                          ☐ Almost new

☐ Kind-of old                       ☐ Brand new

☐ Not too old                       ☐ Other _____

# Secret Place

A secret place in the home that I am moving away from is: _____

_____

_____

(Check One)

☐ I think someone else can find the secret place.

☐ I don't think anyone will EVER find the secret place.

☐ Other_____

_____

_____

# I Never Noticed That Before!

Investigate the home that you are moving away from and find three things that you have never noticed before.

1. _____
_____
_____

2. _____
_____
_____

3. _____
_____
_____

# Floor Plan

On the grid below, draw the floor plan of the home that you are moving away from. You can draw the entire home, or just your room.

# Floor Plan Maze

Can you find your way from the front door to the back door?

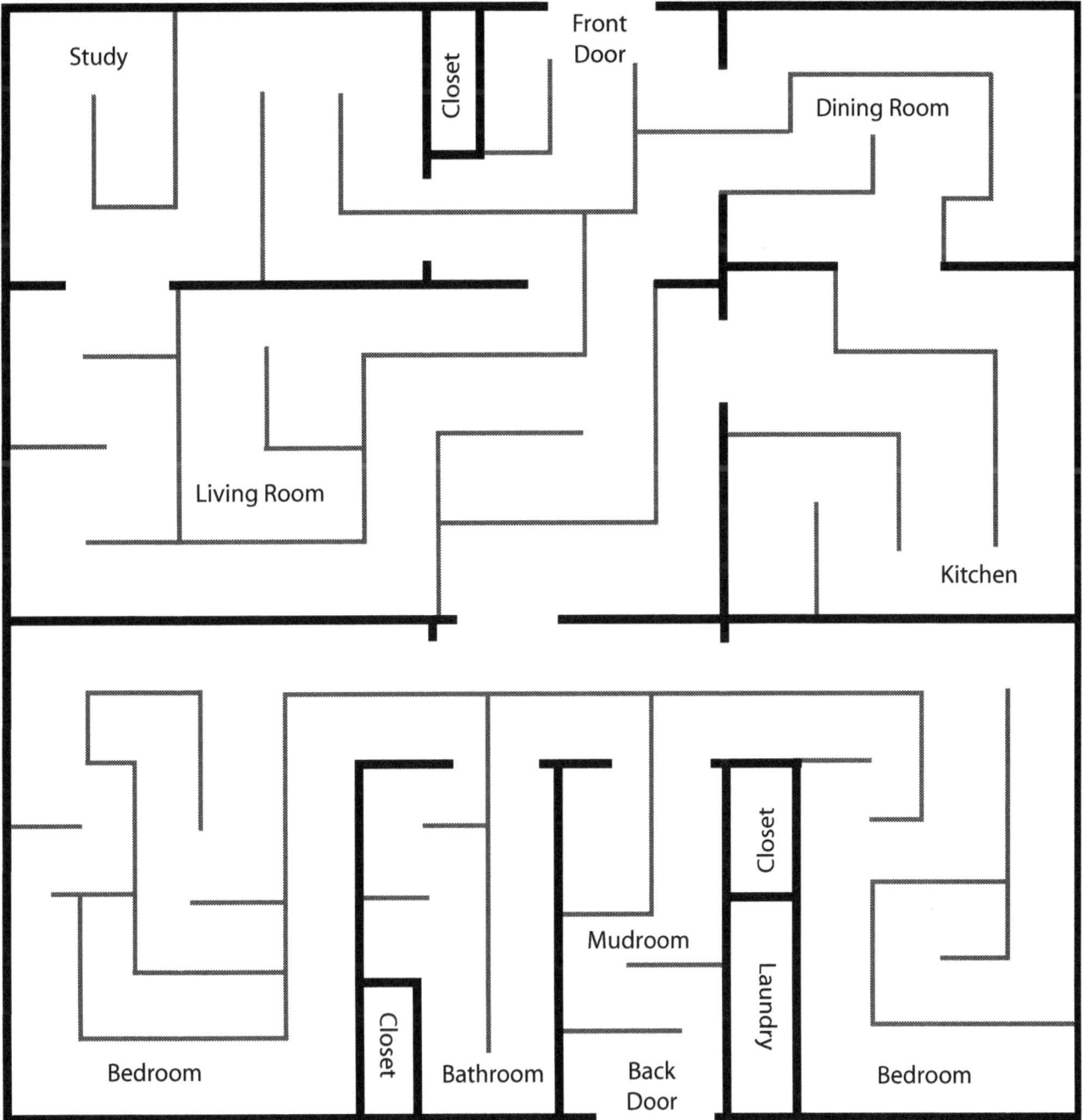

Study

Closet

Front Door

Dining Room

Living Room

Kitchen

Bedroom

Closet

Bathroom

Mudroom

Closet

Laundry

Back Door

Bedroom

# Scrapbook: Where I Lived Before I Moved

Draw pictures or paste photos of the home that you are moving away from.

# Goodbye Home

When I move, I want to say, "Goodbye," to these places in the home that I am moving away from. They are my favorite places.

Inside: _____

_____

_____

_____

_____

_____

_____

Outside: _____

_____

_____

_____

_____

_____

_____

# Memory Stone

1. Find a stone and paint or write on it. Here are some ideas for what you might put on your stone:

> Your name.
>
> How long you lived in the home that you are moving away from.
>
> Important things that happened while you lived in the home.

**TIP!** Write or paint on the stone with something that will last a long time, like a marker used to label moving boxes.

2. What did you write on your memory stone? _____

_____

_____

_____

_____

3. Bury the stone somewhere near your home. If you think the ink might be washed away, wrap it in some plastic first.

(Check One)

☐ I think someone will find the stone in _____ years.

☐ I do not think anyone will ever find the stone.

☐ Other _____.

# Remembering My Schools

I have attended these schools _____

_____

_____

_____

_____

_____

_____

My favorite teachers are _____

_____

_____

_____

_____

My favorite classes are _____

_____

_____

_____

_____

_____

My favorite school activities are _____

_____

_____

_____

_____

_____

# Scrapbook: My Schools

Draw pictures or paste photos of the schools that you have attended while living in the home that you are moving away from. Write the name of each school.

# School Puzzle

Can you find these words and phrases in the word search puzzle?

| | |
|---|---|
| BELL | PAPER |
| BOOKS | PENCIL |
| CLASS | PLAY |
| COMPUTER | PRINCIPAL |
| FOLDER | RECESS |
| FRIENDS | REPORT CARD |
| GET SCHOOL RECORDS | RETURN LIBRARY BOOKS |
| GRADES | SCISSORS |
| GRADUATE | SUMMER READING |
| HOMEWORK | TEACHER |
| LEARN | TEST |
| LESSON PLANS | VACATION |
| LUNCH | YELLOW BUSES |
| NOTEBOOKS | QUIZ |

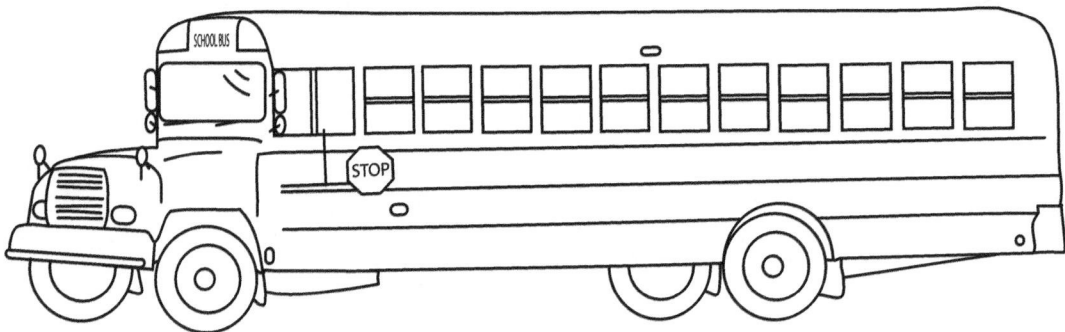

# School Word Search Puzzle

```
R L D Y H C O M P U T E R C H O R B
A E O F P C D C R E C E S S O B E N
X S T A N Z L E A R N Z F T M Y P Q
I S Q U I Z B A E B Y C R F E F O U
P O O G R A D E S A A E I O W S R Z
S N H R P N G F L S Q Z E L O O T E
U P O A R B L P S L D U N D R M C A
M L W D I O U I Z Z R T D E K C A Y
M A N U N K N Q B O O K S R A P R E
E N G A C A C R Q R O Z R E D Z D L
R S X T I X H Y C P A P E R K Z W L
R H M E P L J U M Q R R L X R G E O
E V A C A T I O N E P D Y L T F G W
A I U V L T K T H S I J K B Q U I B
D O L B V J S C I S S O R S O F G U
I V O J W X A C O N M W U X O O H S
N U N O T E B O O K S I H Q P Y K E
G V G E T S C H O O L R E C O R D S
```

# Remembering My Community

Some places in my community that I want to visit one more time before I leave are _____

_____

_____

My favorite places to play are _____

_____

_____

Some places that I go every week are _____

_____

My favorite things to do in the summer are _____

_____

My favorite things to do in the fall are _____

_____

My favorite things to do in the spring are _____

_____

My favorite things to do in the winter are _____

_____

My favorite holiday is _____ .On this holiday, my favorite place to go is

_____

# Community Maze

Follow the gray path from the house (Start) to the park (End).

End

Start

# Leafing, a Pressing Matter

To remember your community, collect some leaves from trees near your home or town. These leaves can be pressed and then saved in this activity journal. To press the leaves, follow these instructions:

You will need: Leaves, Waxed Paper, Scissors, Iron, Ironing Board (Ask a grown-up before using the iron.)

1. Collect leaves that are either fresh from the tree, or fallen leaves. Make sure they are not rotted nor moldy.

2. Cut two pieces of waxed paper for each leaf. The pieces of waxed paper should be larger than each leaf, leaving at least one to two inches all around.

3. Flatten each leaf by pressing it between two sheets of waxed paper and placing a heavy object on each of them.

4. After at least 24 hours, seal the wax around the leaf with an iron on medium to medium-high heat. Place a thin dish towel over the wax paper sheets containing the leaf, and evenly iron until the wax is sealed. When cool enough to touch, flip the sealed leaves over and evenly iron the back-side as well.

5. Once your pressed leaves are cooled, save them carefully. After you have completed this Moving Activity Journal, keep your leaves between these pages.

# My Leaves

# Scrapbook: My Community

Draw pictures or paste photos of places in your community that you have enjoyed while living in the home that you are moving away from.

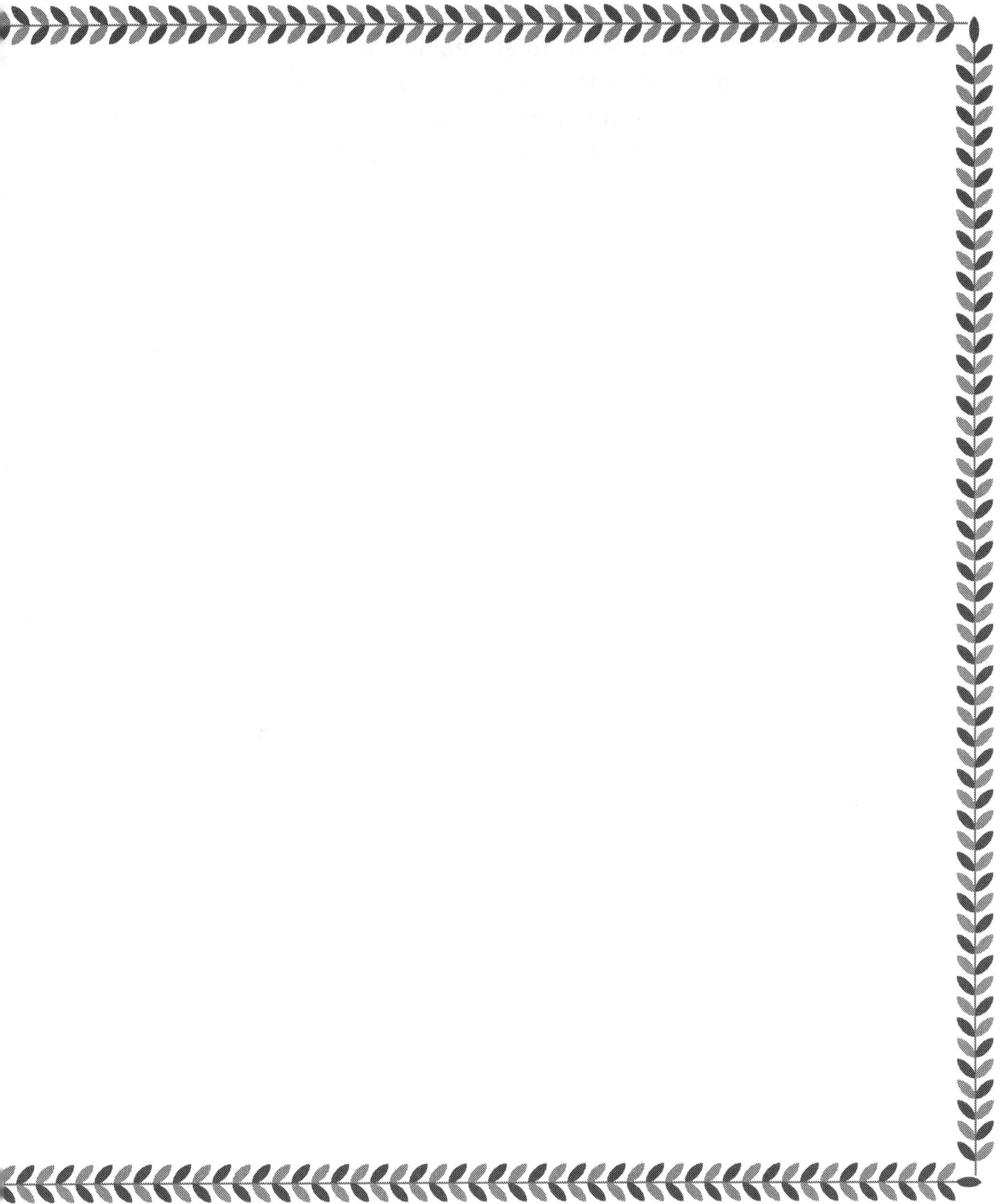

# Our Moving Plans

**Getting Ready**
Moving your home to someplace new,
Making plans and thinking them through,
Learning about where you are moving to,
And when, and how, and what you can do!

Our moving date is _____

I will be traveling by (car, airplane, train, etc.) _____
_____

I am moving to the state of _____

This is near _____
_____
_____
_____

Our new address will be _____
_____

Our new phone number will be _____

# A Good Reason to Move

Check and write about each of the reasons why your family is moving:

☐ New job _____

☐ New school _____

☐ To save money _____

☐ To try new things _____

☐ To be near _____

☐ To be in weather that is _____

☐ To live in a home that is _____

☐ To be closer to my favorite _____

☐ Other _____
_____

☐ Other _____
_____

☐ Other _____
_____

# Geography

Our new home is _____ miles away from the home that I am moving away from "as the bird flies" - which means measuring straight from one place to another in a straight line, not following roads.

Following roads, our new home is _____ miles away from the home that I am moving away from.

These are the directions from my old home to my new home: _____

_____

_____

_____

_____

_____

_____

_____

_____

_____

_____

_____

_____

_____

_____

_____

_____

_____

_____

_____

# Our Route

Here is a map showing how to get to my new home:  (Draw or paste a map showing the route to your new home.)

# Moving Makes Me Feel

Circle the words that describe how you feel about moving. It is okay to circle more than one feeling. You may have big feelings and little feelings at the same time. You may have happy feelings and sad feelings at the same time. This is normal.

**EXCITED**   Anxious   Hopeful

ANGRY   *Happy*   **Confused**

ANNOYED   nervous   *Relieved*

Scared   Sad   CURIOUS

**THRILLED**   CRANKY

Other _____

Other _____

Other _____

**TIP!** If you are sharing this activity journal, more than one person may circle a feeling - then you feel the same way!

# A Few Thoughts About Moving

_____

_____

_____

_____

_____

_____

_____

# I Need a Break!

Moving is a busy time with much to think about. From the list below, circle things that you would like to do when you need to take a break from preparing to move.

Go for a walk

Talk to someone

Go to a park

Exercise

Play

Do something fun that doesn't have *anything* to do with moving.

Learn something new about where I am moving.

Listen to my favorite music

Write a letter to a friend

Fly a kite

Be alone

Take a nap

Read a book

Spin in circles

Talk to _____because he/she always makes me _____

Other _____
_____
_____

Other _____
_____
_____

**TIP!** If you are sharing this activity journal, more than one person can circle the same thing. Maybe you can do that thing together!

# Keys

This is the key to the home that I am moving away from.

(Trace the key.)

This is the key to my new home.

(Trace your new key once you have it.)

40

# My Research

# Resources

There are so many ways to learn about the area where you are moving. Things that help you learn and answer questions are your, "Resources."

Check all of the ways that you would like to discover new things about the area where you are moving.

- [ ] Ask the phone company to send a copy of the local phone book with business pages.

- [ ] Search the Internet.

- [ ] Find books at the library.

- [ ] Talk to _____ because he/she knows a lot about the place that I am moving to.

- [ ] Rent or borrow a movie about the area.

- [ ] Read a map of the area.

- [ ] Other_____

- [ ] Other_____

- [ ] Other_____

Begin to do some of the above things to learn about your new place. These tools will help you fill out this activity journal. Every time you find a "resource" that provides information about your new place, write what it is here. You can use these resources to answer questions later in this activity journal.

_____

_____

_____

_____

_____

_____

_____

# State to State

| | Name the state that you are moving away from: | Name the state that you are moving to: |
|---|---|---|
| Draw or paste a picture of the state flag for each state. | | |
| What is the state capital? | | |
| What is the state flower? | | |
| What is the state animal? | | |
| What is the state bird? | | |
| What is the state dinosaur? | | |
| What is the state fish? | | |
| What is the state fruit? | | |
| What is the state tree? | | |
| What year was the state formed? | | |
| What year did the state join the Union? | | |
| The Governor of the state is? | | |

**TIP!** Not every state will have an answer. For example, some states don't have a state dinosaur. That's okay! Just write "N.A." in the box, for "Not Applicable."

# My New State

Draw a picture of your new state here. Or, if you are moving outside of the United States, draw a picture of your new country here, and list facts and information about your new country.

**TIP!** If you are moving within the same state, only fill in one column on page 42. In your drawing on page 43, draw and label the county that you are moving away from and the new county where you will be moving.

# United States Word Scramble

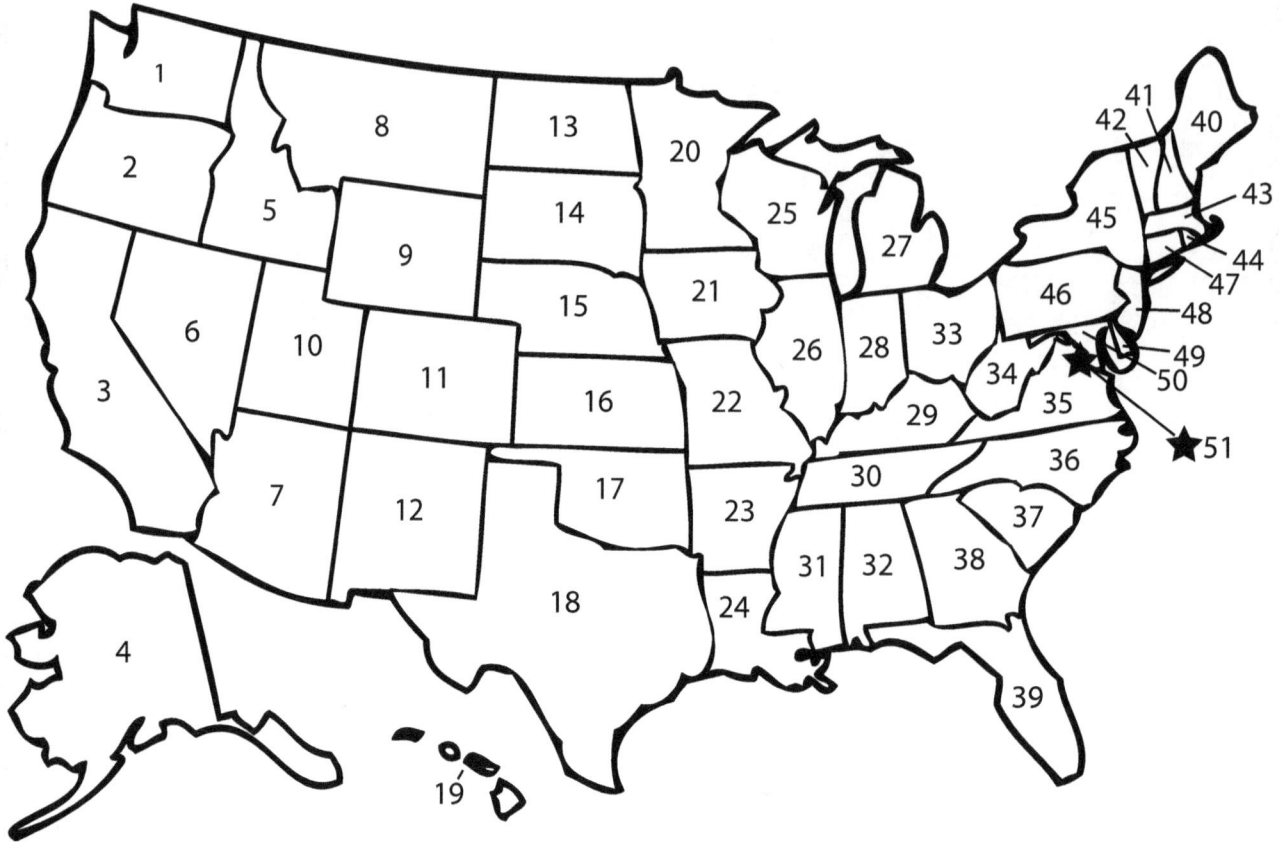

1. SHGIOWTNAN _____

2. ONEOGR _____

3. RIANLIAFOC _____

4. KASLAA _____

5. DOIAH _____

6. VANEDA _____

7. RZOIAAN _____

8. TAMNAON _____

9. YGNMWOI _____

10. THUA _____

11. OCDALOOR _____

12. CEXIWNOME _____

13. TADHTKNROOA _____

_____

14. AOHDOUTATSK _____

_____

15. ABNRSEKA _____

16. SSKNAA _____

17. OAOAHKLM _____

18. ASETX _____

19. IIWHAA _____

20. SIMNNEATO _____

21. OAIW _____

22. SORIMIUS _____

23. AAASRKNS _____

24. ASULANIOI _____

25. IOCNSSIWN _____

26. INOLILIS _____

27. HMGCIIAN _____

28. IDANINA _____

29. KNUTEKYC _____

30. STENESENE _____

31. SSSSPPIIIIM _____

_____

32. ABLAAAM _____

33. HOOI _____

34. ISEVGIAWTRNI _____

_____

35. INGIVIRA _____

36. NRRLANICHOTOA _____

_____

37. OTHALASRNOUCI _____

_____

38. IOGERGA _____

39. LDFOAIR _____

40. EMNIA _____

41. IHWENASHMPRE _____

_____

42. MEONVRT _____

43. SCTEMSATSAHUS _____

_____

44. NLHORSAIDED _____

_____

45. WYEOKNR _____

46. AYLVSNPNIEAN _____

_____

47. TCONICCNEUT _____

_____

48. EEYNWJESR _____

49. ELADAREW _____

50. NALMRYAD _____

51. OICITSTDRFAOLBMCUI _____

_____

# My Home Inspections

Before you move, answer these questions about the home that you are moving away from. After you move, answer these questions about your new home.

| | The home that I am moving away from: | The home that I am moving to: |
|---|---|---|
| What type of building (apartment, condo, new home, old home, etc.): | | |
| Looking out your window, what can you see: | | |
| Number of bedrooms: | | |
| Number of bathrooms: | | |
| Number of windows: | | |
| What color are the carpets? | | |
| Number of toilets: | | |
| Number of lights: | | |
| How many footsteps is it from the front door to your bed? | | |
| How many steps does the home have? | | |
| What is the smallest space in the home? | | |
| What is the biggest room in the home? | | |

| | The home that I am moving away from: | The home that I am moving to: |
|---|---|---|
| How many sinks are in the home? | | |
| How many doors are in the home? | | |
| How many electrical outlets are in the home? | | |
| Name or draw a picture of the plants around the home: | | |
| What color is the soil around the home? | | |
| What is your favorite view from the home? | | |
| When is the growing season? | | |
| Describe the road to your new house: | | |
| Other: | | |
| Other: | | |
| Other: | | |

# Rumor Has It...

Using the table on the next page, list things that you have heard about the place where you are moving. Once you have moved and have learned more about these things, write whether the things that you heard were true, false, or sometimes true.

## Most importantly, what do _YOU_ think?

**Well, I heard...**
I heard the people all are blue.
I heard the sky is always green.
I heard the water tastes like glue,
And smells just like a lima bean.
I heard the schools are filled with goo,
And all the bugs jump, yell, and cheer.
Good thing I don't have to take as true,
The silly rumors that I hear!

| Where I am moving... | After learning more, do you think this is true, sometimes true, or not true? | Most importantly, what do you think? |
|---|---|---|
| ...the weather is: | | |
| ...the people are: | | |
| ...everyone likes to: | | |
| ...the best food is: | | |
| ...everyone wears: | | |
| ...the people talk: | | |
| ... | | |
| ... | | |
| ... | | |
| ... | | |
| ... | | |

# So Much to Look Forward To

**Possibilities**
Searching, Asking, Looking, Reading,
Finding, Hearing, Learning, Leading,
Wondering now, Discovering how,
Growing, Knowing, and Succeeding.

Find the phone numbers, web sites, and addresses for organizations like those listed below that are nearest the new place that you will be living.

Chamber of Commerce _____

_____

Parks and Recreation Department _____

_____

Visitors' Bureau _____

_____

Library _____

_____

Find the names, addresses, and phone numbers for other organizations that seem interesting to you. List them here:

_____

_____

_____

_____

_____

_____

_____

_____

_____

_____

**TIP!** For ideas, look in the phone books, library books, web sites, or other resources that you listed on page 41.

To learn about more fun things to do near your new home, call, e-mail, or write to the organizations that you have listed and ask them to send you information about fun activities.

(Check One)

☐ Information should be sent to the home that I am moving away from because I will still be there for a while.

☐ Information should be sent to my new home because I will be moving soon.

☐ Information should be sent to: _____

_____

_____

# Fun Things to Do Near My New Home

I have discovered these fun things to do near my new home: _____

_____

_____

_____

_____

_____

_____

_____

_____

_____

_____

_____

_____

_____

_____

# Making Myself at Home

| List activities that you have enjoyed near your old home. | Find similar activities near your new home. List them here along with any planning notes. |
| --- | --- |
| | |
| | |
| | |
| | |
| | |
| | |
| | |
| | |
| | |

List 5 things that make you feel like you are at home or that make your home feel extra special to you.

1. _____
2. _____
3. _____
4. _____
5. _____

What are some things that will make you feel this way in your new home?

1. _____
2. _____
3. _____
4. _____
5. _____

What are some ways that _you_ can help make your new place feel like home?

_____
_____
_____
_____
_____
_____
_____
_____
_____
_____
_____

# My New School

The name of my new school is _____

My new school has grades _____ through _____.

The address of my new school is _____

_____

My first day of school will be on (date and day of week) _____

The school colors are _____

The school mascot is _____

I will get to school by _____ (bus, carpool, car, walk, bike, train, etc.)

Directions from my new home to my new school are _____

_____

_____

_____

_____

Directions from my new school back to my new home are (reverse directions) _____

_____

_____

_____

_____

_____

# Visiting My New School

There will be _____ kids in my class.

The principal's name is _____

My new teachers will be _____
_____
_____
_____

Describe the school _____
_____
_____

Describe your classrooms _____
_____
_____
_____

What activities does the school have? _____
_____
_____
_____

What do you see around the school?_____
_____
_____
_____
_____

# Notes About My New School

_____
_____
_____
_____
_____
_____
_____
_____
_____
_____
_____
_____
_____
_____
_____
_____
_____
_____
_____
_____
_____
_____
_____
_____
_____

# Pen Pal

You or your parents can contact your new school before the move and ask the school to recommend a pen pal. Tell the school what you are interested in, and ask the school to contact someone with similar interests. If that person's parents agree, ask that the school provide you with the name, phone number, and address of your pen pal. Before you move, begin writing letters or e-mails back and forth with your pen pal.

My Pen Pal is _____

My Pen Pal's address is _____
_____
_____

My Pen Pal's phone number is _____

My Pen Pal's e-mail address is _____

Both my Pen Pal and I like to _____
_____
_____

Attach an envelope to this page. Save letters
from your pen pal in this envelope.

# Scrapbook: My New School

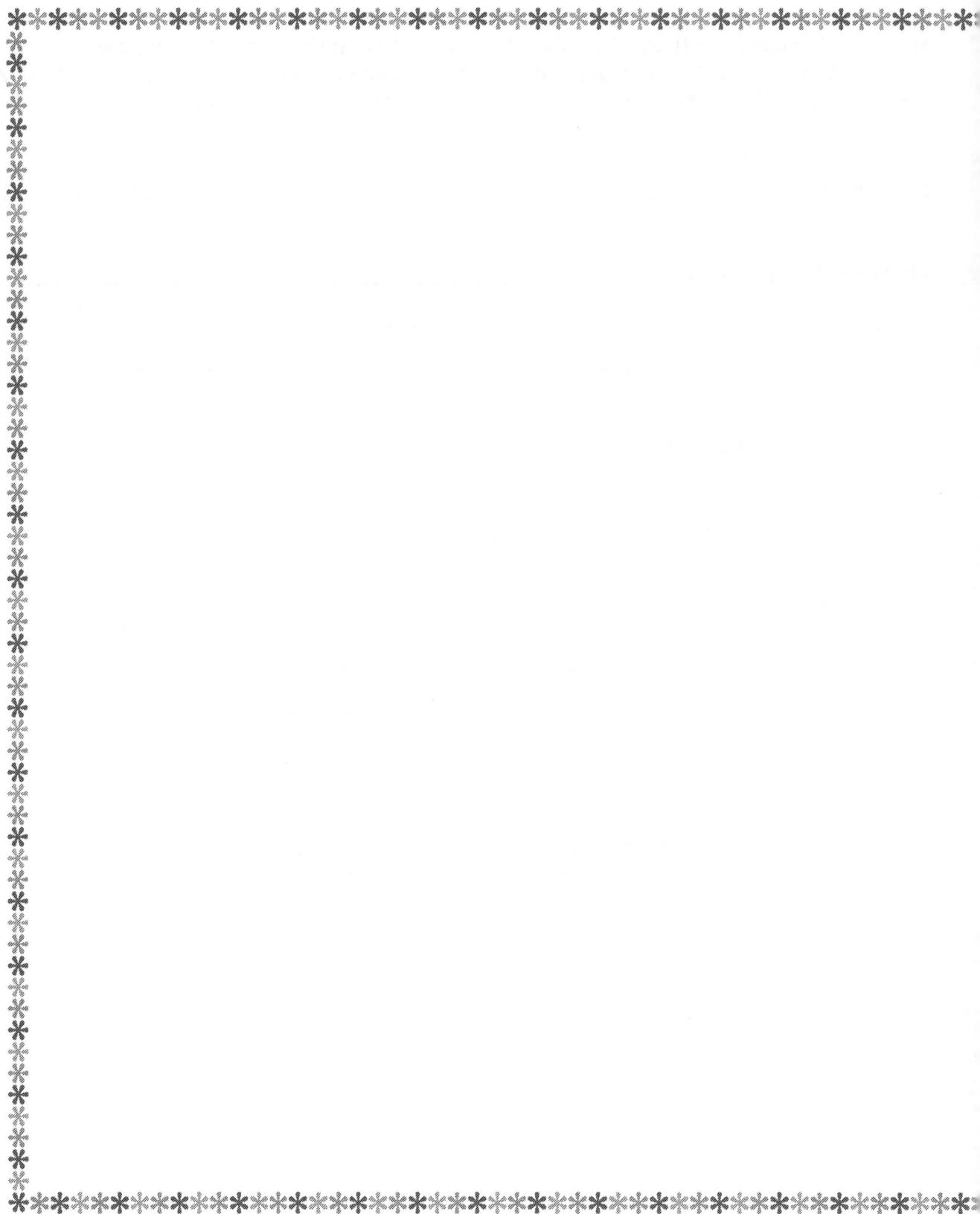

Draw pictures or paste photos of your new school here.

# My New Community

## Making Connections

(Check One)

☐ I already know people who live in my new community.

List them here _____

_____

_____

_____

_____

☐ I don't know anyone who lives in my new community.

List people who might know someone in your new community, such as family, friends, teachers, or coaches._____

_____

_____

_____

_____

_____

Ask the people that you have listed above if they know people in your new community. Take notes here: _____

_____

_____

_____

_____

You or your parent can contact these connections to learn about people and places in your new community.

# People, Places, and Things

A fun place to play near my new home is _____

The library is called _____

  and the library's address is _____

Natural attractions near my new home are _____

_____

_____

A museum near my new home is _____

The movie theatre near my home is called _____

  and the address of the theatre is _____

Some restaurants near my new home are _____

_____

_____

I want to eat at _____ first.

I also want to visit the _____

_____

_____

I will buy groceries at _____

_____

My new doctor will be _____

_____

# Making New Friends

Check-off all of the ways that you would like to meet new friends.

☐ Join an after-school program.

    The after-school program that I am interested in is _____

☐ Play with other kids in my neighborhood.

☐ Play sports. The sports that I like to play are _____

_____

☐ Join a club. The club that I would like to join is _____

_____

☐ Take lessons. I would like to take_____ lessons.

☐ Take classes. I would like to take _____ classes.

☐ Do my favorite hobby. My favorite hobby is _____

_____

☐ Get involved in activities such as _____

_____

☐ Go to a park. I would like to go to a park that has _____

_____

☐ Other _____

☐ Other _____

☐ Other _____

# Friendship Word Scramble

Unscramble these words and then fill-in the sentences below.

(1) lcepais ____ ____ ____ ____ ____ ____ ____

(2) ndki ____ ____ ____ ____

(3) nrigac ____ ____ ____ ____ ____ ____

(4) mmncoo ____ ____ ____ ____ ____ ____

(5) fsea ____ ____ ____ ____

(6) didivaliun ____ ____ ____ ____ ____ ____ ____ ____ ____ ____

Good friends are:

(1) ____ ____ ____ ____ ____ ____ ____ .

...because they are:

(2) ____ ____ ____ ____

and

(3) ____ ____ ____ ____ ____ ____ .

We have things in:

(4) ____ ____ ____ ____ ____ ____

that are fun and:

(5) ____ ____ ____ ____ .

They like me for who I am, because I am an:

(6) ____ ____ ____ ____ ____ ____ ____ ____ ____ ____

# Staying in Touch

### Friends
A friend is like a star,
Shining in the night.
Glowing from afar,
With happy brilliant light.
When the sun sets someplace new,
And old friends are far from near,
The sky above reminds me,
That their love shines brightly here.

# My Friends

After I move, I want to stay in touch with these people: _____

_____

_____

_____

_____

_____

_____

_____

_____

_____

_____

_____

# So Many Ways to Stay in Touch

After you move, there are many ways to stay in touch with friends.

Check all of the ways that you would like to stay in touch with your friends.
I would like to:

- ☐ Write letters to my friends.
- ☐ Call my friends on the telephone.
- ☐ Invite my friends to visit my home.
- ☐ Make change of address cards for my friends.
- ☐ Visit my friends for the weekend.
- ☐ Visit my friends during the summer.
- ☐ Other _____
- ☐ Other _____
- ☐ Other _____

# I Will Remember You When...

Another way to stay close to each of your best friends is to share a "Secret Reminder" with each friend. Your Secret Reminder can be anything that you both will see at each of your homes. Agree that whenever one of you sees the Secret Reminder, you will think of your friend. You might choose a rainbow, a star-filled sky, an animal that you both like, or a basketball slam-dunk. Let your friend help you pick the Secret Reminder. Then, you each promise to think of the other whenever you see your Secret Reminder!

# Goodbye Friends

There are many ways to say, "Goodbye," to your friends.

Check the ways that you would like to say, "Goodbye," and add your own ideas to the list.

☐ Have a farewell party.

☐ Spend the night with each of these friends _____

_____

_____

☐ Have a small party at school.

☐ Get together to play with my friends at _____

_____

☐ Say, "Goodbye," when I see my friends at school or around town.

☐ Give each of my friends paper and a stamped envelope with my new address - that way they can write me after I move.

☐ Other _____

_____

☐ Other _____

_____

☐ Other _____

_____

# Post Office Change of Address

Visit your local Post Office and pick-up a Change of Address form for your family. These forms are used to request that important mail sent to your old address is forwarded to your new address. You pick the date when the Post Office will begin forwarding your mail. Submit the form early to avoid a last-minute rush.

(Check One)

☐ I have submitted my Post Office Change of Address form. The Post Office will begin forwarding my mail on this date: _____

☐ Other _____

_____

_____

# Change of Address Cards

Before you move, make Change of Address cards to hand-out to your friends. Be creative, making the cards in any way that you like. You can hand-write the cards or use a computer. You can use any kind of paper, decorate the cards, or buy pre-printed cards. You will want to have your Change of Address cards ready as you visit with your friends. Include your name, your new address, and if possible, your new phone number or maybe even an e-mail address and the date of your move.

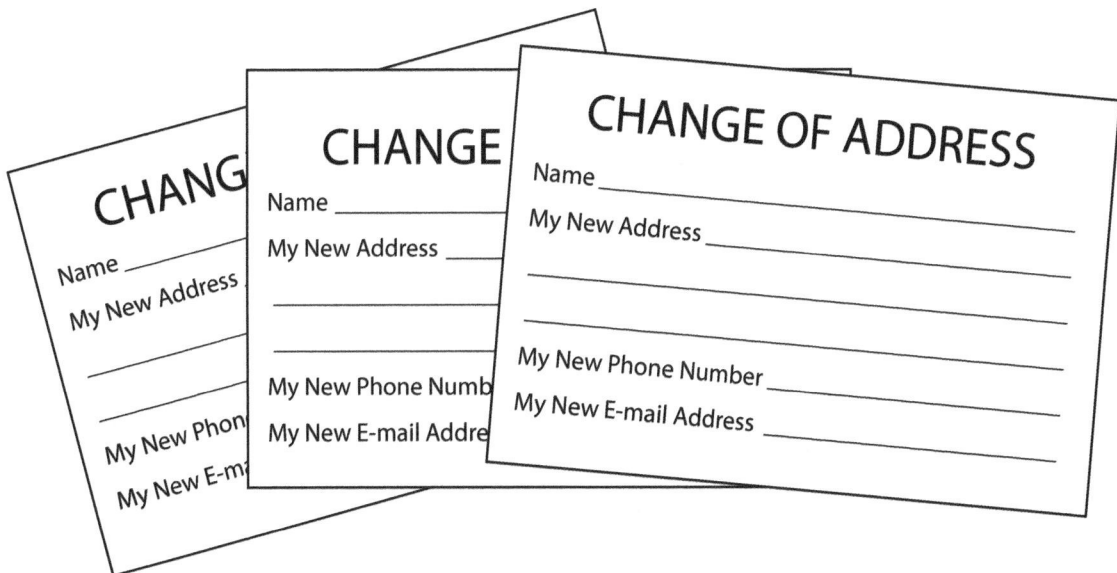

CHANG
Name _____
My New Address _____
_____
My New Phon_____
My New E-m_____

CHANGE
Name _____
My New Address _____
_____
My New Phone Numb_____
My New E-mail Addre_____

CHANGE OF ADDRESS
Name _____
My New Address _____
_____
_____
My New Phone Number _____
My New E-mail Address _____

# To Do: My Friends Checklist

You might be visiting with many of your friends one last time before your move. You might also be visiting with or saying, "Goodbye," to people who have been helpful to you, like teachers, coaches, neighbors, or friends of your family. As you visit with these people, give them your Change of Address cards. Consider taking a camera with you and asking someone to take a picture of you with your friends.

On the next few pages, there are activities to complete as you visit with these important people. You can ask them for their addresses, ask them to write a "Moving Message" in your Moving Activity Journal, and collect photos of your friends. Have your Change of Address cards ready to hand out, and remember each of the things in the checklist below when you see your friends.

## My Friends Checklist

- Give my friend a Change of Address card.

- Ask my friend to write a "Moving Message" in my Moving Activity Journal.

- Get or take a photo of my friend to paste into my Moving Activity Journal.

- Have my friend write his or her address in my Moving Activity Journal address book.

- Other - is there anything else that you want to remember to do when you see your friends?

- _____
- _____
- _____
- _____
- _____
- _____
- _____
- _____
- _____
- _____
- _____

# My Address Book

Your address book is where you write down information about the people that you want to stay in touch with after you move. On these pages, gather information about your friends and other people who are helpful to talk to, like teachers, coaches, neighbors, or friends of your family.

Name _____

Address _____

_____

Home Phone_____

Mobile Phone _____

E-mail _____

Birthday _____

Notes _____

_____


Name _____

Address _____

_____

Home Phone_____

Mobile Phone _____

E-mail _____

Birthday _____

Notes _____

_____


Name _____

Address _____

_____

Home Phone_____

Mobile Phone _____

E-mail _____

Birthday _____

Notes _____

_____


Name _____

Address _____

_____

Home Phone_____

Mobile Phone _____

E-mail _____

Birthday _____

Notes _____

_____

Name _____

Address _____

_____

Home Phone_____

Mobile Phone_____

E-mail _____

Birthday _____

Notes _____

_____

Name _____

Address _____

_____

Home Phone_____

Mobile Phone_____

E-mail _____

Birthday _____

Notes _____

_____

Name _____

Address _____

_____

Home Phone_____

Mobile Phone_____

E-mail _____

Birthday _____

Notes _____

_____

Name _____

Address _____

_____

Home Phone_____

Mobile Phone_____

E-mail _____

Birthday _____

Notes _____

_____

Name _____

Address _____

_____

Home Phone_____

Mobile Phone_____

E-mail _____

Birthday _____

Notes _____

_____

Name _____

Address _____

_____

Home Phone_____

Mobile Phone_____

E-mail _____

Birthday _____

Notes _____

_____

Name _____

Address _____

_____

Home Phone_____

Mobile Phone_____

E-mail _____

Birthday _____

Notes _____

_____

Name _____

Address _____

_____

Home Phone_____

Mobile Phone_____

E-mail _____

Birthday _____

Notes _____

_____

Name _____

Address _____

_____

Home Phone_____

Mobile Phone_____

E-mail _____

Birthday _____

Notes _____

_____

Name _____

Address _____

_____

Home Phone_____

Mobile Phone_____

E-mail _____

Birthday _____

Notes _____

_____

Name _____

Address _____

_____

Home Phone_____

Mobile Phone_____

E-mail _____

Birthday _____

Notes _____

_____

Name _____

Address _____

_____

Home Phone_____

Mobile Phone_____

E-mail _____

Birthday _____

Notes _____

_____

Name _____

Address _____

_____

Home Phone_____

Mobile Phone_____

E-mail _____

Birthday _____

Notes _____

_____


Name _____

Address _____

_____

Home Phone_____

Mobile Phone_____

E-mail _____

Birthday _____

Notes _____

_____


Name _____

Address _____

_____

Home Phone_____

Mobile Phone_____

E-mail _____

Birthday _____

Notes _____

_____


Name _____

Address _____

_____

Home Phone_____

Mobile Phone_____

E-mail _____

Birthday _____

Notes _____

_____


Name _____

Address _____

_____

Home Phone_____

Mobile Phone_____

E-mail _____

Birthday _____

Notes _____

_____


Name _____

Address _____

_____

Home Phone_____

Mobile Phone_____

E-mail _____

Birthday _____

Notes _____

_____

Name _____

Address _____

_____

Home Phone_____

Mobile Phone_____

E-mail _____

Birthday _____

Notes _____

_____

Name _____

Address _____

_____

Home Phone_____

Mobile Phone_____

E-mail _____

Birthday _____

Notes _____

_____

Name _____

Address _____

_____

Home Phone_____

Mobile Phone_____

E-mail _____

Birthday _____

Notes _____

_____

Name _____

Address _____

_____

Home Phone_____

Mobile Phone_____

E-mail _____

Birthday _____

Notes _____

_____

Name _____

Address _____

_____

Home Phone_____

Mobile Phone_____

E-mail _____

Birthday _____

Notes _____

_____

Name _____

Address _____

_____

Home Phone_____

Mobile Phone_____

E-mail _____

Birthday _____

Notes _____

_____

# Moving Messages

Have your friends, relatives, teachers, and other
important people write a Moving Message here.

# Scrapbook: My Friends

Draw pictures or paste photos of the people that
you want to stay in touch with after you move.

# Game: A Funny Letter

Provide a word for each of the categories listed below. You can ask others for words and play this game more than once. Be as silly as you like. You will use these words to complete the letter on the next page. No peaking at the letter! You want to pick the words before you know what the letter says. This is what makes it funny!

1.  A friend's name_____
2.  A feeling _____
3.  A town, city, or state _____
4.  An activity that some people do (ending in 'ing') _____
5.  The name of someone who is moving_____
6.  Another activity that some people do (ending in 'ing') _____
7.  A feeling _____
8.  A word that describes something (adjective) _____
9.  A place that you can go _____
10.  Places that you can go _____
11.  A word that can describe a person_____
12.  Something that you do (verb) _____
13.  Things (noun, plural) _____
14.  A word that describes something (adjective) _____
15.  A number _____
16.  A famous person _____
17.  Something that you do (verb) _____
18.  Another famous person _____
19.  A word that describes something (adjective) _____
20.  Things (noun, plural) _____
21.  Another word that describes something (adjective) _____
22.  Another thing (noun)_____
23.  More things (noun, plural) _____
24.  A person that you know _____
25.  A feeling _____
26.  A thing in a home (noun) _____
27.  Another person that you know _____
28.  A place that you visit _____
29.  A number _____
30.  A thing (noun)_____
31.  A thing that you do (verb) _____
32.  Your name_____

# A Funny Letter

Use the words that you chose on the previous page to fill in the blanks in the letter below. Just match the number of each word with the number of each blank. Then read the letter out loud.

Dear (1) _____,

    I am very (2) _____ to announce that I am moving to

(3) _____. I will be moving as soon as (4) _____ is over

and (5) _____ finishes (6) _____. This move makes

me feel (7) _____ because I will be near a (8) _____,

(9) _____, lots of (10) _____, and (11) _____

people who I like to (12) _____ with.

    My new home is built of (13) _____ so it is very (14) _____.

I have heard that (15) _____ years ago, (16) _____

visited the home to (17) _____ with (18) _____. Also,

the home has (19) _____ (20) _____, a very

(21) _____ (22) _____, and lots of (23) _____.

    (24) _____ is especially (25) _____ about the

new home's (26) _____, and (27) _____ can't wait to

visit a nearby (28) _____. I hope that you will write me (29) _____

times in the next year, and that you will visit before the (30) _____

(31) _____.

                                       Sincerely, (32) _____.

# Packing

**One and All!**
Boxes, boxes, pack it all!
Packing boxes big and small,
Packing boxes short and tall,
Packing boxes wall to wall.
In everyone room, in every hall,
So many boxes, I must crawl!
Fragile boxes must not fall.
Heavy boxes, lift and haul.
Boxes packed by one and all.

My favorite things are coming with me!  The most important things that I am packing are _____

_____

_____

_____

_____

_____

The last things that I want to pack are _____

_____

_____

_____ because they are very important to me!

# Where are My Boxes? Stickers

As you are moving, and when you get to your new home, it might be helpful to easily see which boxes are filled with the things that go in your room. Of course you will write your name on the box. You can also use stickers to identify your boxes, so that they can be easily seen among the stacks of boxes.

Find sheets of stickers for each person who is moving. You may need a few sheets for each person to make sure you have enough. Each person's stickers should be different from everyone else's. For boxes that contain a person's personal things, put one of his or her stickers on *each side* of the box.

In the space below, put one of each person's stickers and write his or her name next to his or her sticker.

TIP! Let others decide what stickers they like for their boxes. Work together, including grown-ups and everyone who is moving, especially others who are keeping their own Moving Activity Journals.

# Labeling Boxes

Check all of the ways that you are going to label your boxes.

☐ Write on the box.

☐ Make stick-on labels.

☐ Buy stick-on labels.

☐ Draw pictures.

☐ Use Stickers

☐ Other_____

☐ Other_____

☐ Other_____

Check all of the notes that you want on your boxes.

☐ The room that the box should go in at the new home.

☐ The contents of the box.

☐ "Fragile," for things that could break.

☐ "This Side Up," for things that should not be tipped over.

☐ Other_____

☐ Other_____

☐ Other_____

☐ Other_____

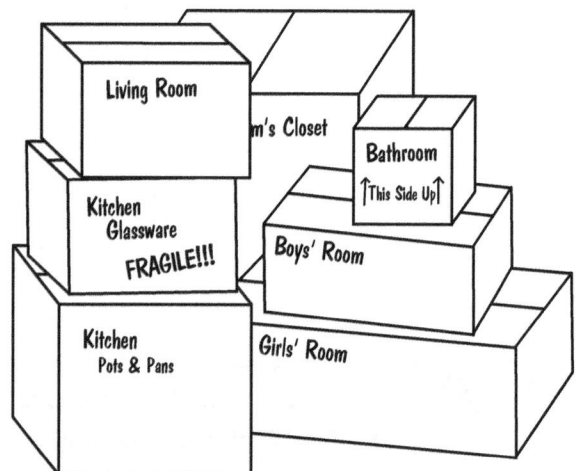

# That's My Most Important Box!

As you are moving, and when you get to your new home, it might be helpful to easily see those *few* boxes that contain your *most important* things. Of course you will write your name on all of your boxes and maybe even put stickers on each of them. You can also create an easy-to-draw and easy-to-see symbol for marking one or two of your *most important* boxes.

Draw your very own symbol or picture here, and then put this symbol or picture on the top and sides of your *most important* boxes.

**TIP!** Make your symbol or picture simple so that you can easily draw it many times. Really little kids may only be able to draw something as simple as a red circle, for example. That's a great way for them to see their contributions and be reassured of where their *most important* things are.

# Pack Facts

The most fragile things that I am packing are _____

_____

_____

_____

_____

Something that I can not put in a box is _____

Something that I want to carry to my new home is _____

Some things that I don't need anymore are_____

_____

_____

_____

The biggest thing that I am moving is_____

The smallest thing that I am moving is _____

The smelliest thing that I am moving is_____

The newest thing that I am moving is _____

The oldest thing that I am moving is_____

The bounciest thing that I am moving is _____

The hairiest thing that I am moving is _____

The softest thing that I am moving is_____

The sharpest thing that I am moving is_____

The lightest thing that I am moving is _____

The heaviest thing that I am moving is _____

The longest thing that I am moving is_____

The coldest thing that I am moving is_____

The most colorful thing that I am moving is _____

The most messy thing that I am moving is_____

The wettest thing that I am moving is _____

The silliest thing that I am moving is _____

The stickiest thing that I am moving is_____

The most yummy thing that I am moving is _____

The noisiest thing that I am moving is _____

The shiniest thing that I am moving is _____

The scariest thing that I am moving is _____

The brightest thing that I am moving is _____

# My Packing Plan

This Packing Plan helps organize everyone who is part of your moving "team." Work together. Guess the number of boxes that you will need, and after you have packed, have fun counting how many boxes you actually used! Most people usually end up needing more boxes than they thought!

| These are the rooms and spaces that have things to pack: | These are the people who will help pack things in the room or space. | I am guessing that this room or space will require this many boxes. | After you are done packing, count the actual number of boxes used. Write the number here. |
|---|---|---|---|
|  |  |  |  |
|  |  |  |  |
|  |  |  |  |
|  |  |  |  |
|  |  |  |  |
|  |  |  |  |
|  |  |  |  |
|  |  |  |  |

**TIP!** Work together on this plan, including grown-ups and everyone who is moving, especially others who are keeping their own Moving Activity Journals.

| These are the rooms and spaces that have things to pack: | These are the people who will help pack things in the room or space. | I am guessing that this room or space will require this many boxes. | After you are done packing, count the actual number of boxes used. Write the number here. |
|---|---|---|---|
| | | | |
| | | | |
| | | | |
| | | | |
| | | | |
| | | | |
| | | | |
| | | | |

# Packing by Definition

Each of the words or phrases below are important packing terms. In your own words, write what each of these packing words means or why they are important when moving. Ask around and write other people's answers, then, share your answers. Sharing your ideas is part of working together, and learning other people's ideas can be very interesting.

Box _____

Donate _____

Fragile _____

Gentle _____

Gift _____

Give _____

Help _____

Label _____

Lift at Knees _____

Moving _____

Pack _____

Protect _____

Sort _____

Stack _____

Take a Break _____

Tape _____

Team _____

This Side Up _____

Throw Out _____

Wrap _____

# Packing Word Search Puzzle

Can you find these words in the word search puzzle?

| Box | Give | Pack | Tape |
|-----|------|------|------|
| Donate | Help | Protect | Team |
| Fragile | Label | Sort | This Side Up |
| Gentle | Lift at Knees | Stack | Throw Out |
| Gift | Moving | Take a Break | Wrap |

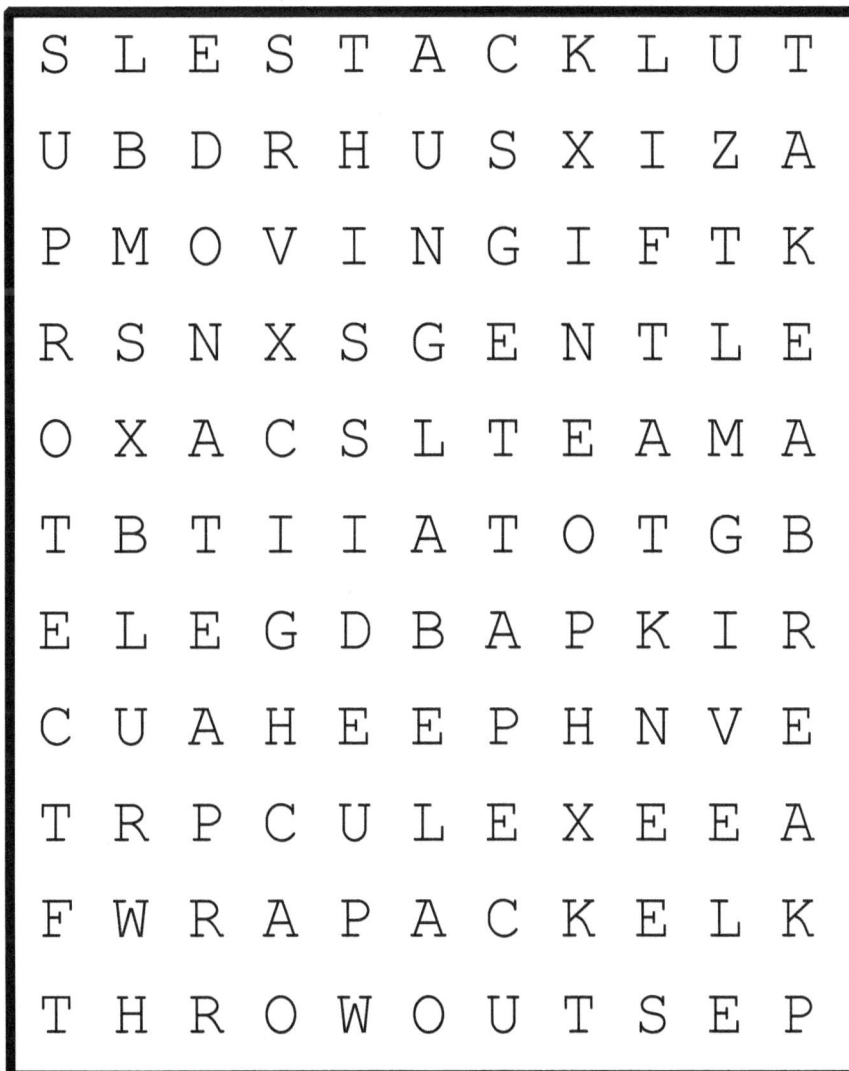

```
S  L  E  S  T  A  C  K  L  U  T
U  B  D  R  H  U  S  X  I  Z  A
P  M  O  V  I  N  G  I  F  T  K
R  S  N  X  S  G  E  N  T  L  E
O  X  A  C  S  L  T  E  A  M  A
T  B  T  I  I  A  T  O  T  G  B
E  L  E  G  D  B  A  P  K  I  R
C  U  A  H  E  E  P  H  N  V  E
T  R  P  C  U  L  E  X  E  E  A
F  W  R  A  P  A  C  K  E  L  K
T  H  R  O  W  O  U  T  S  E  P
```

# Packing My Moving Bags

There are some things that you can not put away in boxes. You will need these things during your move and as soon as you arrive in your new home. Let's figure out what goes into your Moving Bags!

My Moving Bags will have: (Check all that apply, and try to not put too much in your moving bags. Most things can be packed.)

☐ My favorite small toy or game _____

☐ My favorite book_____

☐ My favorite craft or hobby _____

☐ My favorite music _____

☐ My favorite jewelry_____

☐ My Moving Activity Journal

☐ My favorite blanket

☐ My glasses or contact lenses

☐ My toothbrush and toothpaste

☐ My hairbrush or comb

☐ A hair dryer

☐ My shampoo and soap

☐ My favorite towel

When I arrive in my new home, the weather will be (Check One):

☐ really hot          ☐ kind-of-warm          ☐ really cold

☐ very warm          ☐ cool                   ☐ totally freezing

so I better bring my _____

_____

I will also need to pack clothes. This is what I need (enter the number of each item that you will need, enter '0' if you do not need something).

_____long-sleeved shirts          _____pajamas

_____short-sleeved shirts          _____sweaters

_____pants                         _____sweatshirts

_____shorts                        _____other_____

_____pairs of underwear            _____other_____

_____pairs of socks                _____other_____

_____bras                          _____other_____

_____pairs of shoes                _____other_____

_____jackets                       _____other_____

_____bathing suits                 _____other_____

When it is time to pack my Moving Bags, I am going to put all of this stuff in my _____

_____

_____

_____

Notes _____

_____

_____

_____

# Family Moving Bags

There are some family things that can't be packed away in boxes. The family might need these things during the move and as soon as the family arrives in its new home. Let's figure out what to put in your Family Moving Bags!

My Family Moving Bags will have (Check all that apply):

☐ Sleeping Bags _____

☐ Favorite Pillows_____

☐ Toilet Paper _____

☐ Shower Curtain_____

☐ Cleaning Supplies _____

☐ Vacuum_____

☐ First Aid Kit_____

☐ Medical Records _____

☐ Medicines_____

☐ School Records_____

☐ Pet Records _____

☐ Pet Food_____

☐ Other Pet Supplies _____

_____

☐ Family Treasurers_____

_____

☐ Other_____

_____

☐ Other_____

_____

☐ Other_____

_____

☐ Other_____

_____

**TIP!** This plan involves the whole family. Work together, including grown-ups and everyone who is moving, especially others who are keeping their own Moving Activity Journals.

# Packing Ideas

When packing, you will need to wrap items so that they don't break or get scratched. By re-using soft items from around the house, you can save money, use fewer boxes, and reduce the amount of trash that you create.

Circle all of the things that you will save or set-aside and use as padding around fragile items.

Newspaper (don't use on things that might get stained by the ink, or wrap these items in a plastic grocery bag first!)

Extra Clothes

Extra Pillows

Packing Paper

Throw Pillows

Tissue Paper

Blankets

Plastic Grocery Bags

Stuffed Animals

Paper Grocery Bags

Extra Clothes (wrap in plastic bags to protect from dampness, snags, etc.)

Bubble Wrap

Other_____

Foam Packing Peanuts (after your move, some shipping stores will take these and re-use them).

Smaller Boxes

Other_____

Old T-shirts

Other_____

Old Towels

Other_____

# Jobs for Packing Helpers

There are many important jobs that need to be done when packing. These jobs can be shared by a few, done by everybody, or one person can be chosen to become the "expert" at doing that job. Here are just a few ideas. Can you think of any more?

| Packing Job | This job will be done by: |
|---|---|
| **The Hardware Taper** - Some things that get packed have screws or other hardware that you don't want to loose. Tape the screws or other hardware to the item being packed. If an item has lots of hardware, you might want to put the hardware in an enclosed plastic bag or envelope first. This way, you will have the hardware ready when you unpack. Only put tape and hardware where it won't damage the item, like on the bottom or backside. | |
| **The X-er** - Use masking tape to tape a large "X" across all pictures and mirrors that are being packed. Ask someone to carefully hold the item for you, so that you don't hurt yourself or damage the item. Use a type of tape that is easily removed from the item. (Specialty boxes are available for safely packing pictures and mirrors.) | |
| **Packing Peanut Manager** - When foam packing peanuts are needed, you're on the job!  When someone needs packing peanuts, they can ask you for help. Use a plastic pitcher or large cup or container as a scoop. Don't forget to pick-up any packing peanuts that fall outside of the box - they can be saved for the next box. | |
| **Caution Captain** - Boxes that are fragile must be labeled, "FRAGILE," on the top and each side. These and other boxes may also need to be labeled, "THIS SIDE UP," for safe moving. You can be the person ready to put these cautionary labels on the box. You can either write the words in large, easy to read letters, or buy or make sick-on labels. | |
| | |

**TIP!** Work together on this, including grown-ups and everyone who is moving, especially others who are keeping their own Moving Activity Journals.

| Packing Job | This job will be done by: |
|---|---|
|  |  |
|  |  |
|  |  |
|  |  |
|  |  |

# Safe Packing Word Scramble

Unscramble these words and then fill-in the sentences below.

       (1) sneke ____ ____ ____ ____ ____

       (2) motbot ____ ____ ____ ____ ____ ____

       (3) opt ____ ____ ____

       (4) legiraf ____ ____ ____ ____ ____ ____ ____

When lifting something heavy, always bend at the:

       (1) ____ ____ ____ ____ ____

When stacking boxes, put the bigger and heavier ones on the:

       (2) ____ ____ ____ ____ ____ ____

       and put the smaller and lighter ones on the:

       (3) ____ ____ ____

When packing things that break, always wrap them carefully, and label the box:

       (4) ____ ____ ____ ____ ____ ____ ____

# Safety First
# Emergency Information

An emergency contact during my move is _____

If there is an emergency, these people might also need to be contacted _____

_____

_____

_____

A phone number where people can reach me during the move is _____

_____

My doctor's name is _____

My doctor's phone number is _____

Something important that a doctor might want to know about me is_____

_____

_____

It will take _____ days to move.

While I am moving, I will be staying at these places:

_____ Phone Number _____

_____ Phone Number _____

_____ Phone Number _____

_____ Phone Number _____

_____ Phone Number _____

# My Moving Safety Card

Make a safety card that lists all of the important safety information on page 97.

1. Use a note card or cut a piece of paper into a roughly 4 inch by 6 inch card.

2. On the top front of the card, write "My Moving Safety Card."

3. On the front of the card, write the following information:

    Your name

    The names of the people who are moving with you, and how they are related to you.

    Your old address.

    Your new address.

4. On the back of the card, write all of your answers to the "Emergency Information" questions on the previous page.

5. Keep your card in Your Moving Bag, which you will keep near you during the move, or another safe place that you will have access to while traveling.

# Pets on the Move

(Check One)

☐ I am moving with _____ pets.

☐ I am not moving with any pets.

☐ I am finding a new home for my pets.

☐ Other_____

If you have pets, write their names and what kind of animal they are.

_____

_____

_____

_____

_____

_____

_____

# Scrapbook: My Pets

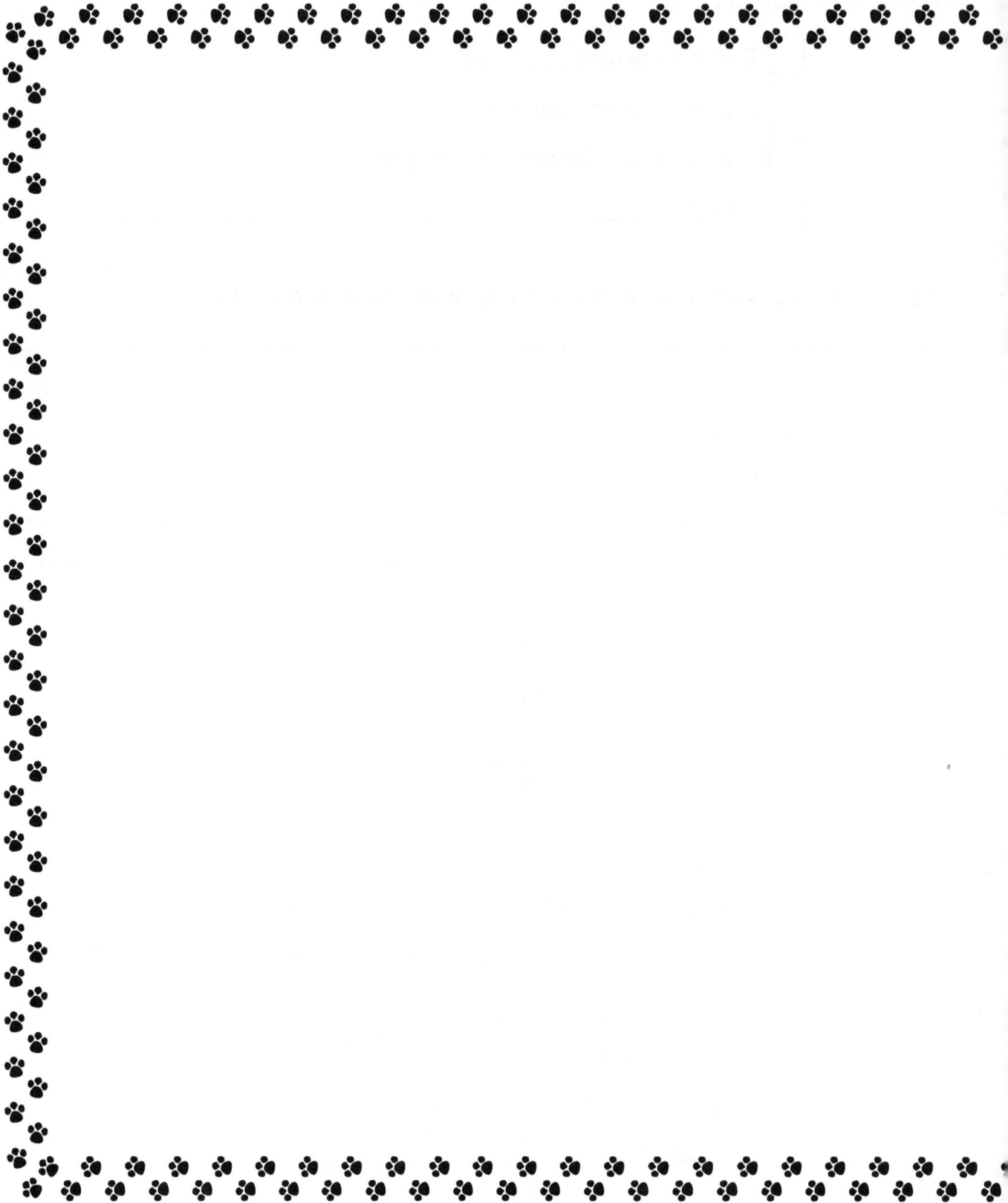

Draw pictures or paste photos of your pets.

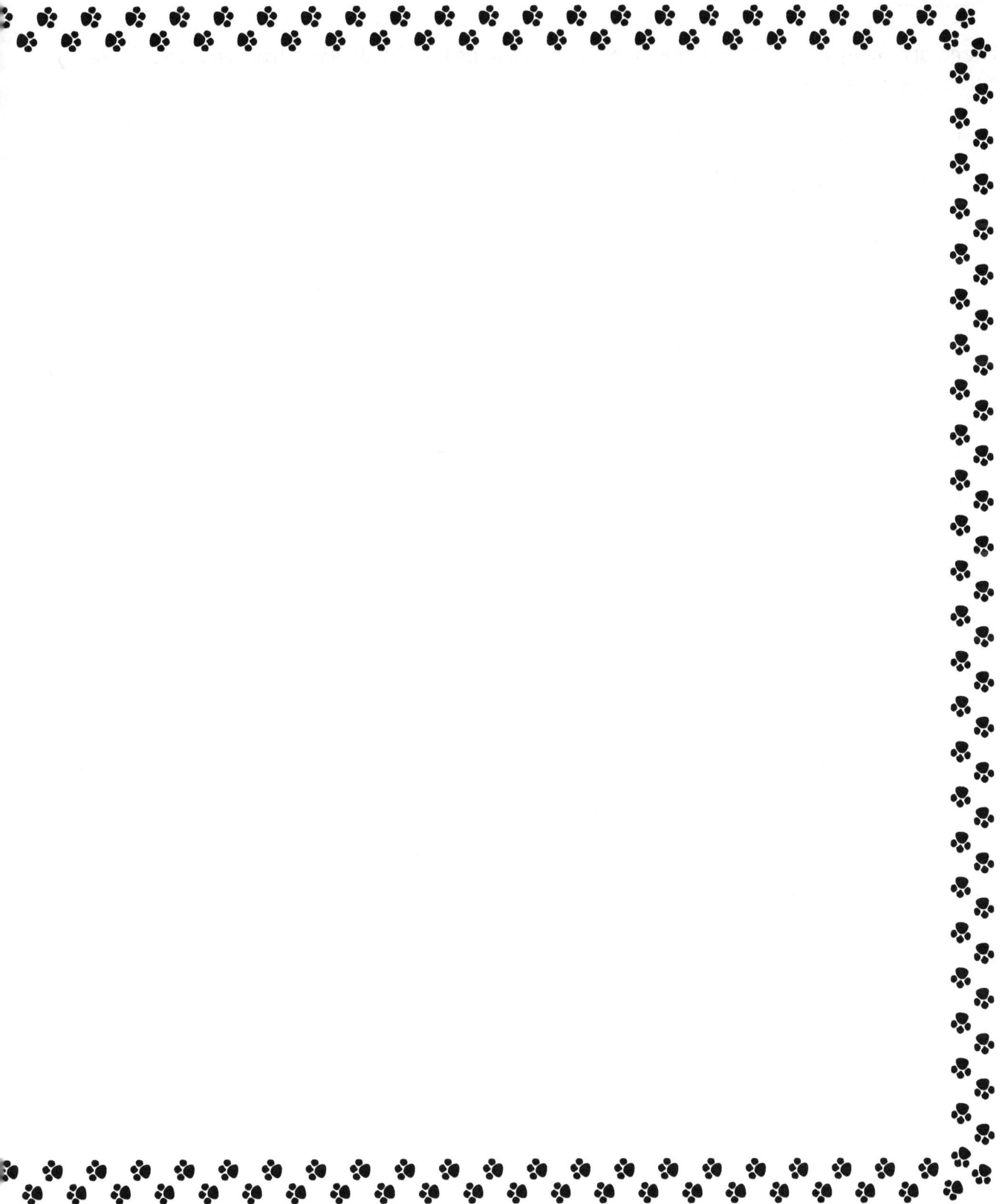

# Pets Moving to a Different Home

This page is for people who can not take their pets to their new home and are finding a different home for their pets.

There are many ways to find new homes for your pets. Check ways that you would like to find a new home for your pet:

☐ Ask family, friends, and neighbors.

☐ Put an ad in the newspaper.

☐ Post flyers around town.

☐ Talk to your veterinarian and post flyers at his or her office.

☐ Use the help of a local animal shelter.

☐ Other _____

☐ Other _____

☐ Other _____

☐ Other _____

List ways that you would like to stay in touch with your pet _____

_____

_____

_____

_____

_____

_____

_____

# Pet Facts

To help your pet feel happy and loved with a new owner in its new home, complete this activity to introduce your pet  Or, if you are able to take your pet with you, complete this activity to create an information sheet that you can attach to your pet's kennel during the move.

On a sheet of notebook or similar sized paper, paste a picture of your pet. Answer the following questions about your pet, writing the answers on the pet's sheet. If you have more than one pet, create an information sheet for each of your pets.

My name is _____ I am a _____

I am _____ years old. My favorite food is _____

I like my food served _____ times a day at these times _____

_____

(Check One or more)

☐ I like to be petted on my _____ .

☐ I don't like to be petted on my _____ .

☐ I don't like to be petted anywhere, please don't pet me.

My favorite game is _____

My favorite place to play is _____

My favorite place to sleep is _____

(Check One, then put only that information on your information sheet.)

☐ I like to go outside.

☐ I do not go outside.

☐ I only go outside when _____ .

☐ Other _____

I will feel very at home if you _____

Some things that I do NOT like are _____

Some things that I do really like are _____

Other important information _____

# Moving Pets

If you are moving with pets, these activities will help you plan your pet's move.

# Pet Tags

It is very important that your pet has a tag with its name and phone number as well as a current rabies tag. This helps the pet find its way to its new home if it accidentally gets separated from you.

Consider making a tag for your pet that has your pet's name and a phone number where someone can reach you during and after your move. This will help keep your pet safe. Many pet stores have tag machines or sell write-on tags.

A phone number where people can reach me during and after the move is_____

_____

# Planning Ahead

Does the city and or state where you are moving require that you have current vaccination records for your pet?_____

_____

Does the city where you are moving require that you buy a license for your pet? _____

_____

If your pet will be traveling using public transportation, such as an airplane, bus, or train, does the carrier require that you make a reservation for your pet or have current vaccination records for your pet?_____

_____

Notes _____

_____

**TIP!** If you are moving with a pet, set aside an extra T-shirt that you can sleep in the night before you move. After sleeping in the shirt, it will smell like you. During your travels, place the shirt in the pet's cage or kennel. Having your familiar scent will comfort the pet. Don't pick a favorite T-shirt, just in case your pet stains or damages the shirt!

# Moving Day!

## Moving Day Job # 1 - Double Check

You have an important job to do!  Now that everything is packed and it is almost time to go, you want to make sure nothing gets left behind. You can "double check."  Look carefully through your home to make sure you have packed everything that you are taking with you. Don't forget to look in these places, checking them off as you go.

_____ Kitchen cabinets and drawers

_____ Bathroom cabinets and drawers

_____ Any other cabinets and drawers (list them) _____

_____

_____ Bedroom closets

_____ Coat closets

_____ Storage closets

_____ Shelves

_____ Attic

_____ Garage

_____ Basement

_____ Storage Shed

_____ Underneath porches and decks

_____ Balconies

_____ Other _____

_____ Other _____

_____ Other _____

_____ Other _____

# Moving Day Job # 2 - My Things

Remember those bags that you packed to carry with you during your move? Now is the time to double check that your Moving Bags are packed and ready to go. Your lists of items to pack are on pages 90 through 93. After you have packed your bags, you can help load them into the car, bus, train, or plane.

# Moving Day Job # 3 - Goodbye Walk

On Moving Day, lead your family on a walk through and around the home that you are leaving. As you walk, visit each of the places that you listed in "Goodbye Home" on page 22. In each place, remember what made it feel like home. Say, "Goodbye," to each of these places, and know that you are taking the feeling of "Home" with you. If you like, read the poem below during your walk.

### Home
Home is where the heart is,
Where my love fills every space.
Home is full of memories,
That moving won't erase.
Home is in the people,
That catch me during falls.
Home is in the air,
And not just within these walls.
Home is like a shadow,
It will always follow me.
And so it is, after I move,
Home is where I'll be.

# What I Did the Day We Left

# While Traveling - Some Things to Think About
# Planning Box Crafts

After you move in and unpack, you will have *lots* of boxes left over. From the following list, check the fun things that you would like to do with some of these boxes, and add your own ideas.

☐ Build a fort                 ☐ Make a costume

☐ Build a puppet theatre       ☐ Other_____

☐ Go cardboard sledding        ☐ Other_____

Now that you have decided what you are going to do with some of those boxes, write or draw your ideas here:

That was fun!  But there will still be a *lot* of boxes left over. Circle any ideas for what you would like to do with all of those extra boxes.

☐ Recycle Them                 ☐ Other_____

☐ Save Them                    ☐ Other_____

☐ Offer them to other families  ☐ Other_____
   who are moving.

# Traveling Maze

Hurry to catch your airplane!  Travel from the boat (Start), to the car, to the airplane (End).

END

START

# Traveling Word Scramble

Unscramble these words and then fit them into the sentences below.

(1) livrgtaen _____ _____ _____ _____ _____ _____ _____ _____ _____

(2) pys _____ _____ _____

(3) setqisoun _____ _____ _____ _____ _____ _____ _____ _____ _____

(4) getixnic _____ _____ _____ _____ _____ _____ _____ _____

(5) nfu _____ _____ _____

(6) raujnol _____ _____ _____ _____ _____ _____ _____

There are lots of fun things to do while:

(1) _____ _____ _____ _____ _____ _____ _____ _____ _____

We can play I-:

(2) _____ _____ _____

and twenty:

(3) _____ _____ _____ _____ _____ _____ _____ _____ _____

We can talk about new things to do near our new home that are:

(4) _____ _____ _____ _____ _____ _____ _____ _____

and:

(5) _____ _____ _____

And we can work on our moving activity:

(6) _____ _____ _____ _____ _____ _____ _____

# Traveling Word Search Puzzle

Can you find these words in the word search puzzle?

| | | | |
|---|---|---|---|
| Adventure | Fresh Start | Moving | State |
| Arrive | Go | New Home | Town |
| Discover | Journey | Relocate | Transfer |
| Explore | Leave | Route | Traveling |
| Find | Map | Search | Trip |

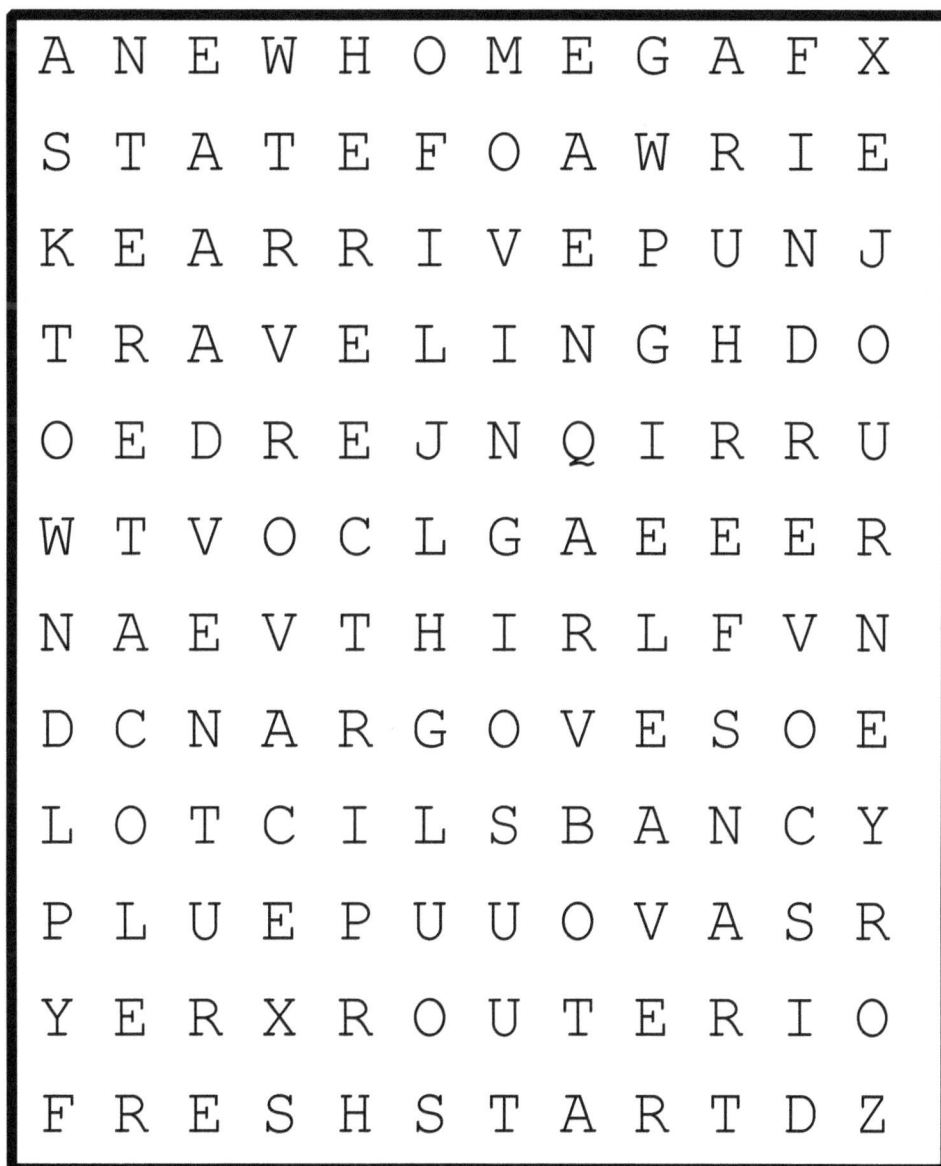

```
A  N  E  W  H  O  M  E  G  A  F  X
S  T  A  T  E  F  O  A  W  R  I  E
K  E  A  R  R  I  V  E  P  U  N  J
T  R  A  V  E  L  I  N  G  H  D  O
O  E  D  R  E  J  N  Q  I  R  R  U
W  T  V  O  C  L  G  A  E  E  E  R
N  A  E  V  T  H  I  R  L  F  V  N
D  C  N  A  R  G  O  V  E  S  O  E
L  O  T  C  I  L  S  B  A  N  C  Y
P  L  U  E  P  U  U  O  V  A  S  R
Y  E  R  X  R  O  U  T  E  R  I  O
F  R  E  S  H  S  T  A  R  T  D  Z
```

# Traveling Observations

While I was traveling, I saw: (list items for each category)

Something tall _____

Something short _____

Something really bright _____

Something really sparkly _____

Something tiny _____

Something huge _____

Something loud _____

Something funny _____

Something that spins _____

Something fuzzy _____

Something beautiful _____

Something famous _____

Something with water in it _____

Something with fire as part of it _____

Something spooky _____

Something red _____

Something orange _____

Something yellow _____

Something green _____

Something blue _____

Something purple _____

Something fast _____

Something slow _____

My favorite things that I saw were _____

_____

_____

You probably won't see an example of every item, and that's okay.  Have fun looking!

# Game: A Funny Story

Provide a word for each of the categories listed below. You can ask friends and family members for words, and play this game more than once. Be as silly as you like. You will use these words to complete the letter on the next page. No peaking at the letter! You want to pick the words before you know what the letter says. This is what makes it funny!

1. The place that you are moving to _____
2. A word that describes something (adjective) _____
3. Another word that describes something (adjective) _____
4. A thing (noun) _____
5. Something that you do (verb) _____
6. A thing that you are traveling with (noun) _____
7. Something that you do (verb) _____
8. Something else that you do that ends with "ing" (verb - ing) _____
9. Someone that you know _____
10. Something that you do that ends with "ing" (verb - ing) _____
11. A word that describes something (adjective) _____
12. A city, town, or state _____
13. A thing (noun) _____
14. A word that describes something (adjective) _____
15. A thing (noun) _____
16. Something that you do (verb) _____
17. A thing (noun) _____
18. A number _____
19. A word that describes something (adjective) _____
20. A thing (noun) _____
21. A word that describes something (adjective) _____
22. A thing (noun) _____
23. A word that describes something (adjective) _____
24. The name of a person traveling with you _____
25. A thing (noun) _____
26. A city, town, or state _____
27. The name of a person traveling with you _____
28. A thing (noun) _____
29. A job title _____
30. A thing (noun) _____
31. Something that you do (verb) _____
32. A word that describes something (adjective) _____

# My Funny Story

Use the words that you chose on the previous page to fill in the blanks in the letter below. Just match the number of each word with the number of each blank. Then read the letter out loud.

On our way to (1) _____, something (2) _____ happened. We

came across a (3)_____ (4) _____ that wanted to (5) _____ our

(6) _____. We tried to get it to (7) _____ but it just kept

(8) _____. That is when we decided we better call (9) _____, who

made everything better by (10) _____.

We took a (11) _____ detour through (12) _____ because

we wanted to see the (13) _____. That was the (14) _____ part

of our trip. It reminded me of the (15) _____when it would

(16) _____ on the (17) _____. I hope to see it again

(18) _____ times.

We stopped to get something to eat at the (19) _____

(20) _____. The food was (21) _____. We ate

(22) _____. It was so (23) _____, (24)_____

asked for the recipe. The secret ingredient is (25) _____.

We had one problem in (26) _____ when (27) _____ lost

the (28) _____. We called a local (29) _____ who found it in a

(30) _____. Next time, we will have to (31) _____ to make sure

that doesn't happen again!

All in all, it was a very (32) _____ trip!

# Moving Travels

I traveled to my new home via (car, plane, bus, etc.)_____

_____

It took _____ days to move.

During the move, the weather was _____

_____

Our Route:  On the Way, I passed through  _____

_____

_____

...and I saw _____

_____

_____

List any unexpected problems along the way _____

_____

_____

_____

How did you solve those problems?_____

_____

_____

_____

Something new that I learned is_____

_____

_____

# Arriving

**A Moving Pro!**
You've done it!  You got here!
You moved!  You've arrived!
You packed, taped,
       pushed and pulled,
Be proud of all you've tried!
Watch out neighbors!
       Here you come,
A mover on the go.
You planned, learned,
       asked and found,
Now you're a moving pro!


We arrived in our new home on this date _____

The weather was _____

Now that we are here, I feel _____
_____
_____

I can't wait to _____
_____
_____

I want to send my friends a picture of _____
_____
_____

# My Moving Story

What happened on the day of your move?  What did you see along the way?  Were there any surprises?  What happened when you arrived at your new home?  Write your moving story here.

_____

_____

_____

_____

_____

_____

_____

_____

_____

_____

_____

_____

_____

_____

_____

_____

_____

_____

_____

_____

_____

_____ _(Continued)_

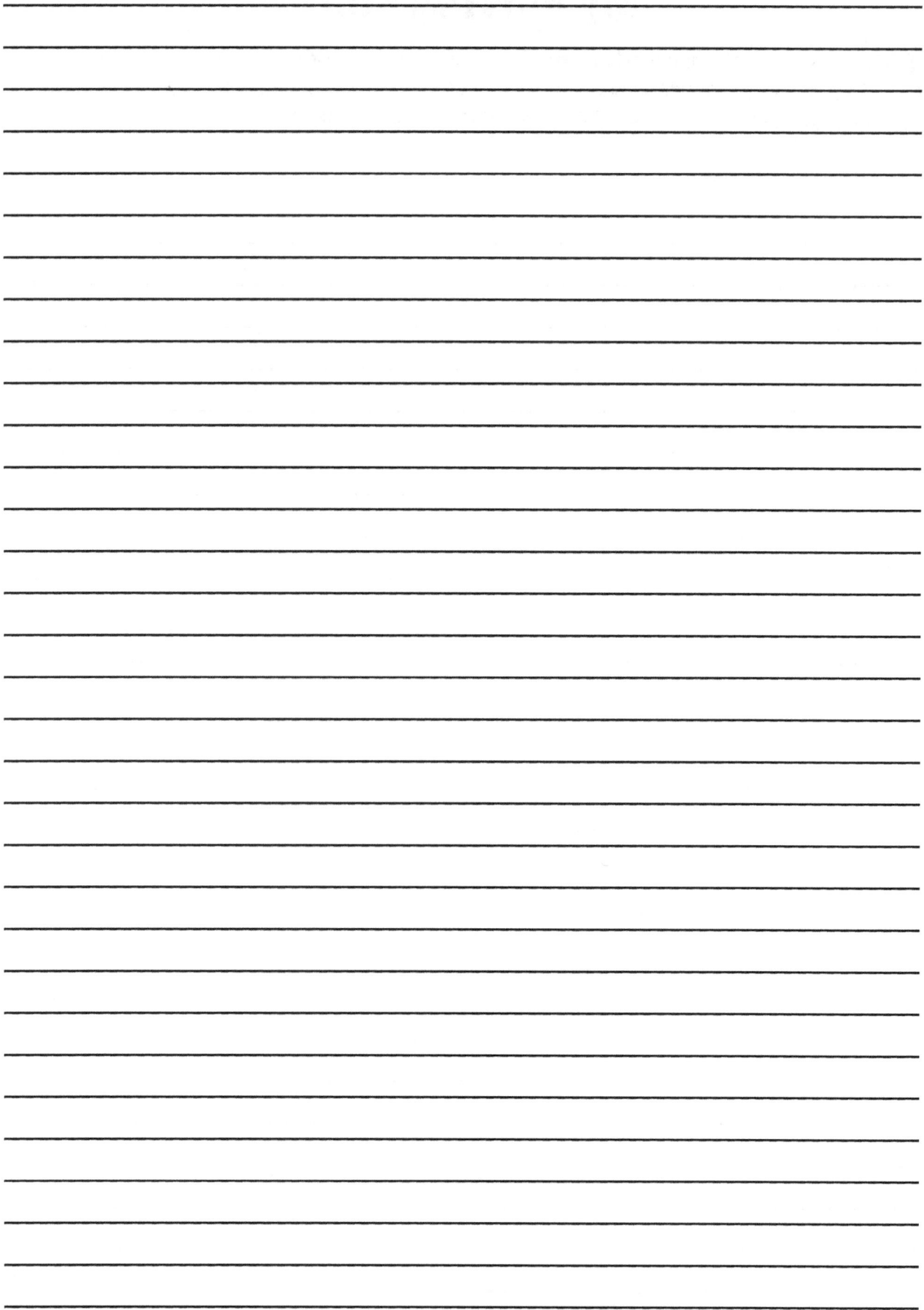

# A Picture is Worth a Thousand Words

Draw a picture or paste a photo of something funny or interesting that happened during your moving travels.

# Settling In

List 5 things about your new home that you are noticing for the first time:

1. _____
2. _____
3. _____
4. _____
5. _____

My Decorating Ideas _____

_____

_____

_____

_____

_____

_____

_____

_____

Guess what I found in my new home! _____

_____

_____

_____

_____

_____

Oops!  Guess what broke during the move! _____

_____

_____

_____

# Discovering My New Home

As you get to know your new home, find places to do each of the following things. As you find places, write them here:

Walk _____

_____

Play _____

_____

Meet People _____

_____

Be Alone _____

_____

See Something Beautiful _____

_____

Help Someone _____

_____

Read a Book _____

_____

Hide _____

_____

See Really Far Away _____

_____

Do my favorite hobby _____

_____

By the way, my favorite hobby is _____

_____

I also discovered these new places in and around my new home _____

_____

_____

_____

_____

# All Five Senses

When I walk around the home barefoot, it feels _____

When I stand outside, I smell _____

When I wake-up in the morning, I hear_____

When I flush the toilet, it sounds_____

When I drink the water, it tastes _____

When I look at the home with my eyes squinty, it looks_____

I like the way the _____smells.

A really interesting sound that I can hear in my new home is _____

_____

The ceilings in my new home feel _____

A smell that I have never smelled before is _____

The smallest thing that I see in my new home is _____

The first meal that I ate in my new home tasted_____

    By the way, my first meal was _____

When I turn the heat on in my new home, it smells _____

Something that makes a humming sound in my new home is _____

The darkest part of my new home is_____

    and the brightest part is_____

The most fun thing in my new home is_____

# A New Perspective

Find a place in your new home where you can safely see your home upside down, like a bed, a sofa, or a chair. Be careful and ask for help if you need it. When you are upside down, what new things do you see that you never noticed before?

_____

_____

_____

_____

_____

_____

_____

_____

_____

# Reminder

Now that you are in your new home, don't forget to complete these activities:

**Trace the Key** to your new home, on page 40.

**My Home Inspections**, on pages 46 and 47.

**Rumor Has it**, on page 48 and 49.

Make your **Box Crafts**, planned on page 108.

Also, remember your ideas from:

**Fun Things to Do Near My New Home**, on page 51.

**Making Myself at Home**, on pages 52 and 53.

# The History of My New Home

Our new home was built in the year _____.

It is _____ years old.

Our new home is (Check One):

☐ Very old                    ☐ Almost new

☐ Kind-of old                 ☐ Brand new

☐ Not too old                 ☐ Other _____

The house was built by_____

List all of the people who have lived in the home. You might want to look at the title documents that came with the house, or ask a landlord about the history of the house, or ask neighbors and people around town if they remember who lived in the house before you did. _____

_____

_____

_____

_____

_____

_____

_____

Our neighbors are _____

_____

_____

_____

_____

_____

_____

Some things that my neighbors have told me about my new home are _____

_____

_____

_____

_____

_____

_____

_____

_____

_____

_____

_____

_____

_____

_____

_____

_____

_____

_____

_____

_____

_____

_____

_____

_____

_____

# Neighborhood Hunt

### Neighborhood Adventure
Searching the neighborhood, clue after clue,
An adventure in someplace that's new to you.
Wondering where foot paths will lead you to,
And finding your very own favorite new view.
Discovering fun things that you can do,
Exploring the neighborhood new to you.

Find a medium paper bag or small box (decorate it if you like). Then, go for a walk around your neighborhood and see if you can find the things listed below and on the next page. If the item is something that you can keep, collect it in your bag or box. Describe the things that you find.

☐ Three different shapes of leaves_____

☐ Two different colored stones _____

☐ A twig_____

☐ Something red _____

☐ Something blue_____

☐ Something yellow _____

☐ Something orange _____

☐ Something green_____

☐ Something purple _____

☐ Something white_____

☐ Something black _____

☐ Something old_____

☐ Something new _____

☐ Something tiny _____

What animals did you see while you were walking around your neighborhood? _____

_____

_____

_____

_____

_____

_____

Take a photo of the things that you collected during your neighborhood hunt and paste the photo below. Or, draw a picture of the things that you collected or saw.

# A Trip Around Town

The first time that I traveled around my new town, I traveled via (car, plane, train, etc.):_____

_____

The weather was _____

Something that I had never seen before is _____

_____

_____

List the interesting places that you saw as you traveled around your new town_____

_____

_____

_____

_____

_____

Some things that are really different from my old town are _____

_____

_____

_____

Some things that are the same as my old town are _____

_____

_____

_____

Some places that I want to visit in my new town are _____

_____

_____

# Notes About My New Town

_____

_____

_____

_____

_____

_____

_____

_____

_____

_____

_____

_____

_____

_____

_____

_____

_____

_____

_____

_____

_____

_____

_____

_____

_____

_____

# Post Cards

As you explore your new town and discover new places, purchase post cards to send to your friends. Use the post cards to tell friends about your move and to let them know that you are thinking of them. Buy one post card for yourself and attach it below. Years later, you can see if your new town looks the same.

I sent post cards to these friends:

_____

_____

_____

_____

_____

_____

_____

_____

_____

My Favorite Post Card of My New Town

(Attach Here)

# What I Have Learned

If we ever move again, we definitely need to remember to _____

_____

_____

_____

My advice for other people who are moving is _____

_____

_____

_____

Something that I thought I would miss, but now that I am here, I don't really miss is

_____

My favorite thing about my new home is _____

_____

_____

_____

Some things that I have learned about myself are _____

_____

_____

_____

_____

I would like to wait _____ years before I move again.

When I grow-up, I think I will probably move _____ times.

# End Notes

You have now completed a really big move! And you have learned a lot along the way. You have special memories from the past, and you have much to discover about your new home. You might still be having some big feelings about your move. Use this space to write whatever you like as you continue along your Moving Journey!

_____

_____

_____

_____

_____

_____

_____

_____

_____

_____

_____

_____

_____

_____

_____

_____

_____

_____

_____

_____

_____

_____

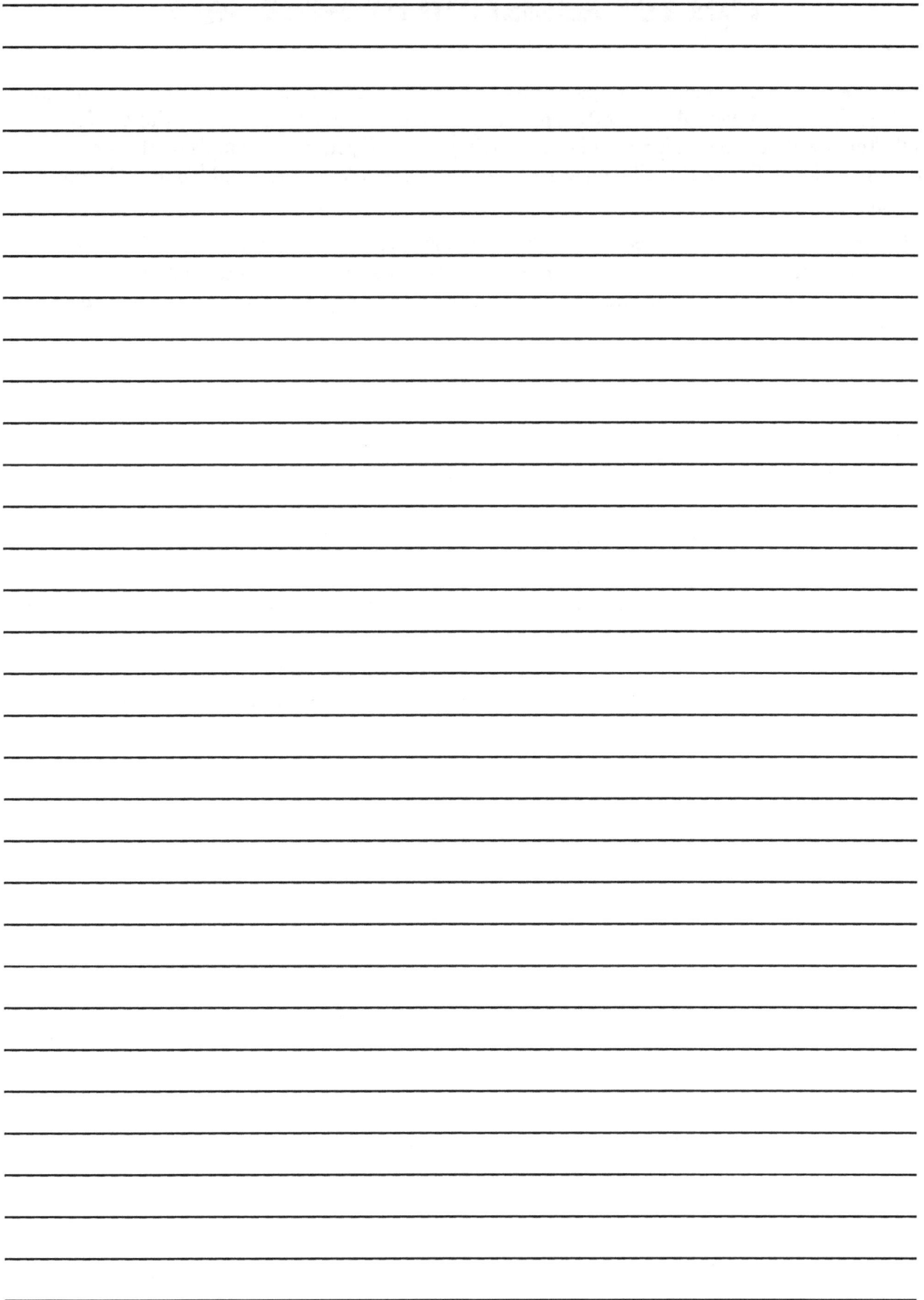

# Tips for Assisting Pre-readers

Read the activities, poems, and questions to the child. Consider making time in your daily routine for the Moving Activity Journal so little movers don't get lost in the shuffle. Your talks will be very helpful and encouraging, even if you don't complete the entire activity journal. Enjoy the silly answers! Your child will look back and laugh at them as well some day.

A few activities may be beyond your child's ability. You can skip these activities, use their ideas for discussion, or enjoy them yourself when you need a break! Look for the many helpful moving tips throughout the journal. They might be helpful for your own planning.

Coloring - Your child can use crayons or markers to color the drawings throughout the journal.

Journal Questions - Read the questions and talk about them with your child. If time allows, write the child's answers. Encourage your child to draw, cut-and-paste pictures, or express his or her thoughts in whatever way he or she enjoys.

Explore Pages (magnifying glass pages) - These activities are fun for a pre-reader to do with a grown-up or older child's assistance, and serve as entertaining breaks from the sometimes hectic pace of preparing to move.

Sharing an Activity Journal - For craft and scrapbook activities, provide your children with loose paper to do these activities on, then paste the crafts in the activity journal or simply keep the loose sheets within the pages of the activity journal.

Floor Plan pg. 18 - Your child can use this page to draw anything that he or she likes or to simply color the squares in his or her own way. Can your child draw a picture of his or her room or a favorite thing in the room?

Scrapbooks pgs. 20, 25, 32, 58, 76, and 100 - Follow the instructions to the best of your child's abilities.

Mazes pgs. 19, 29, and 109 - Encourage your child to give the maze a try, perhaps using a finger to find his or her way instead of a pen or pencil.

Memory Stone pg. 23, Leafing, a Pressing Matter pg. 30, and other Crafts - Work together on these, finding parts that your child can help with or do independently.

Word Search Puzzles pgs. 27, 89, and 111 - Some pre-readers will enjoy looking for the words, even if they can't read them yet. For others, pick one or two words that are meaningful, like your child's name or a favorite thing. Then, your child can search the puzzle for just each letter in the word or words. Can your child count the number of each letter that he or she found?

**Keys pg. 40** - Follow the instructions to the best of your child's abilities.

**My New State pg. 43 and United States Word Scramble pg. 44** - On page 44, have your child color-in the state that you are moving away from and the state that you are moving to. Can your child count the number of states that you will pass through to get from one to the other? Looking at your new state on pg. 44, can your child draw a picture of the state? If so, paste the picture on page 43. Otherwise, on page 43 your child might draw a picture of the place where he or she would like to live.

**Word Scrambles pg. 44, 63, and 96** - Save these for parents - you need to take fun breaks too.

**Change of Address Cards pg. 67** - Grown-ups need change of address cards too. Consider buying, making, or computer printing plain change of address cards and then letting your child decorate the cards and, if able, stamp the envelopes for you.

**My Address Book pg. 69** - Consider using this to help your child learn some early reading skills, like letter and number recognition, phonics, or whatever suits your child's current interests and abilities. Using the space provided, write the first name of a few of your child's favorite friends. Then, write each friend's phone number and birthday. Can your child practice recognizing names, dialing numbers on a pretend phone, or figuring out if anyone has birthdays in the same month? You might allow your child to pick a certain number of friends to call and say, "Hello," to after the move. This could be a special reward for being brave and helpful during the move as well as a proud moment as he or she dials the numbers by his- or herself.

**Moving Messages pg. 74** - Let your child's friends draw small pictures here.

**A Funny Letter pg. 78 and A Funny Story pg. 113** - Save these for the whole family when grown-ups can help. Let your child choose words to the best of his or her abilities, helping as needed. Then, enjoy the funny stories.

**Jobs for Packing Helpers pg. 94** - Pre-readers love to help, especially when there is a lot going on, like a busy move. Guide your child to jobs that suit his or her interests and abilities.

**KEEP JOURNALING SAFE AND FUN** - Remind young journalers of all important rules that need to be remembered when completing these activities, like asking before going outside or using scissors, only using glue in certain areas, or waiting for a parent before meeting new neighbors, and so on. You know your children, home, and move the best, so modify any activities as appropriate and use common sense precautions.

# Answers

## School Word Search Puzzle pg. 27

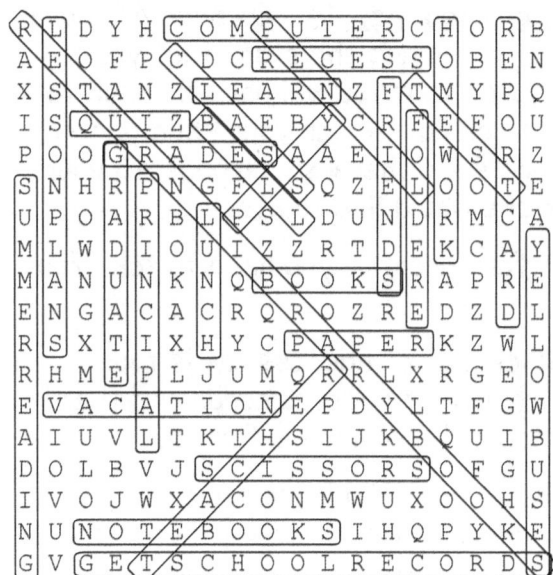

```
R L D Y H C O M P U T E R C H O R B
A E O F P C D C R E C E S S O B E N
X S T A N Z L E A R N Z F T M Y P Q
I S Q U I Z B A E B Y C R F E O U U
P O O G R A D E S A A E I O W S R I
S N H R P N G F L S Q Z E L O O T Z
M P O A R B L P S L D U N D R M C E
M L W D I O U I Z Z R T D E K C A A
E A N U N K N O B O O K S R A P R Y
N G A C A C R Q R O Z R E D Z D L E
R S X T I X H Y C P A P E R K Z W L
R H M E P L J U M O R R L X R G E L
E V A C A T I O N E P D Y L T F G O
A I U V L T K T H S I J K B Q U I W
D O L B V J S C I S S O R S F G U B
I V O J W X A C O N M W U X O O H S
N U N O T E B O O K S I H Q P Y K E
G V G E T S C H O O L R E C O R D S
```

## United States Word Scramble pg. 44

1. Washington, 2. Oregon, 3. California, 4. Alaska, 5. Idaho, 6. Nevada, 7. Arizona, 8. Montana, 9. Wyoming, 10. Utah, 11. Colorado, 12. New Mexico, 13. North Dakota, 14. South Dakota, 15. Nebraska, 16. Kansas, 17. Oklahoma, 18. Texas, 19. Hawaii, 20. Minnesota, 21. Iowa, 22. Missouri, 23. Arkansas, 24. Louisiana, 25. Wisconsin, 26. Illinois, 27. Michigan, 28. Indiana, 29. Kentucky, 30. Tennessee, 31. Mississippi, 32. Alabama, 33. Ohio, 34. West Virginia, 35. Virginia, 36. North Carolina, 37. South Carolina, 38. Georgia, 39. Florida, 40. Maine, 41. New Hampshire, 42. Vermont, 43. Massachusetts, 44. Rhode Island, 45. New York, 46. Pennsylvania, 47. Connecticut, 48. New Jersey, 49. Delaware, 50. Maryland, 51. District of Columbia.

## Friendship Word Scramble pg. 63

Good friends are (1) special because they are (2) kind and (3) caring. We have things in (4) common that are fun and (5) safe. They like me for who I am, because I am an (6) individual.

## Packing Word Search Puzzle pg. 89

```
S L E S T A C K L U T
U B D R H U S X I Z A
P M O V I N G I F T K
R S N X S G E N T L E
O X A C S L T E A M A
T B T I I A T O T G B
E L E G D B A P K I R
C U A H E E P H N V E
T R P C U L E X E E A
F W R A P A C K E L K
T H R O W O U T S E P
```

## Safe Packing Word Scramble pg. 96

When lifting something heavy, always bend at the (1) knees. When stacking boxes, put the bigger and heavier ones on the (2) bottom and put the smaller and lighter ones on the (3) top. When packing things that break, always wrap them carefully, and label the box (4) fragile.

## Traveling Word Scramble pg. 110

There are lots of fun things to do while (1) traveling. We can play I-(2) spy and twenty (3) questions. We can talk about new things to do near home that are (4) exciting and (5) fun. And we can work on our moving activity (6) journal.

## Traveling Word Search Puzzle pg. 111

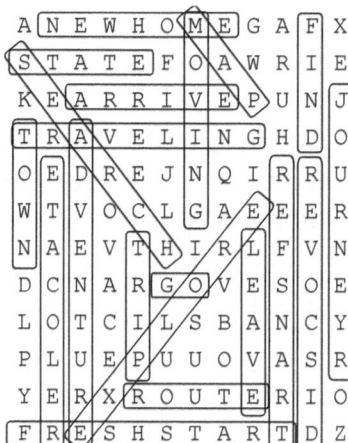

```
A N E W H O M E G A F X
S T A T E F O A W R I E
K E A R R I V E P U N J
T R A V E L I N G H D O
O E D R E J N Q I R R U
W T V O C L G A E E R R
N A E V T H I R L F V N
D C N A R G O V E S O E
L O T C I L S B A N C Y
P L U E P U U O V A S R
Y E R X R O U T E R I O
F R E S H S T A R T D Z
```

# Acknowledgements

I would like to thank these people who helped me with my move, my Moving Activity Journal, and making moving exciting and fun:

_____

_____

_____

_____

_____

_____

_____

_____

_____

_____

**Soaring Kids**

Share your experience! Soaring Moon Books would like to hear from you. With your parent's permission, please e-mail your comments and moving accomplishments, stories, photographs, or drawings to soaringkids@soaringmoon.com.

**And, visit our Kid's Page at www.soaringmoon.com!**

www.ingramcontent.com/pod-product-compliance
Lightning Source LLC
LaVergne TN
LVHW061335060426
835511LV00014B/1933